THE SACRED REVIVAL

MAGIC, MYTH & THE NEW HUMAN

KINGSLEY L. DENNIS

Beautiful Traitor Books

Copyright © 2020 by Kingsley L. Dennis

All rights reserved. No part of this book may be reproduced or transmitted in any form or by any means, graphic, electronic, or mechanical, including photocopying, recording, taping, or by any information storage or retrieval system, without the permission in writing from the publisher.

This edition published by Beautiful Traitor Books
http://www.beautifultraitorbooks.com/

Revised Edition 2020

First edition published by Select Books (2017)

ISBN: 978-1-913816-03-2

Cover Concept: Kingsley L. Dennis & Ibolya Kapta
Cover Design & Book Formatting: Ibolya Kapta

Copyright 2020 by Beautiful Traitor Books.
All rights reserved.
info@beautifultraitorbooks.com

CONTENTS

INTRODUCTION
The World We See ... 1

1. RE-ENCHANTING THE WORLD:
Where There Is Grace and Wonder ... 11

2. COMING AROUND AGAIN:
The Flows and Fluxes of History ... 27

3. SEEKING OUR MYTHOLOGIES:
Where Did All the Gods Go? ... 47

4. JUGGLING WITH SACRED TOTEMS:
Modernity and Beyond ... 67

5. HERE BE DRAGONS:
From Posthistoric to Posthuman ... 85

6. MODERN FICTIONS:
Chaos, Superheroes, and Outer Spaces ... 107

7. NEON TRIBES:
Ecstatic Highs, Techno-Trance, and Digital Gnostics ... 127

8. I SCRATCH YOUR BACK, YOU SCRATCH MINE:
A New Communion in Communication ... 147

9. A SENSE OF THE SACRED:
Magic Never Died ... 163

10. MOON RIVER:
A New Sacred Marriage of the
Masculine and Feminine — 177

11. THE NEW HERETICS:
Shedding the Monkey Mind — 195

12. LIVING THE IMAGINAL:
Dreaming the World into Being — 213

13. OTHERWORLDING:
Or a Re-souling of the Anima Mundi — 225

14. BLACK SANDS:
High Science as Practical Magic — 241

15. SEEKING SALVATION:
Re-defining our Technologies — 263

16. SACRED RESONANCE:
Coherence as the Cosmic Driver — 283

17. COSMIC HUMANISM:
Caretakers for the Sacred Order — 303

EPILOGUE
The Lighthouse — 316

INTRODUCTION

THE WORLD WE SEE

The world we see is the myth we are in.
– Patrick Harpur, **The Philosopher's Secret Fire**

What the universe becomes depends on you.
– Henryk Skolimowski, **A Sacred Place to Dwell**

The book that you now hold in your hands is like a patchwork quilt: Its various colors and textures took many months to come together and form a coherent tapestry. The seed idea for this book had been with me for over a year, nestling deep within my interior, seeking nourishment — and time.

The book initially started out as something different, focusing on the need for re-enchantment (which eventually became the first chapter). Then another form of inspiration gradually unfolded within me, and I began taking notes, scribbling down ideas, passages, and whole paragraphs. After some time, I had various files in my folder, many of them scattered with notes and quotes.

Rather than working in a linear way, from one chapter to the next, as I had done with my previous books, I began writing into different chapters in a lateral way. For example, one of the earliest chapters I wrote ended up near the end of the book, and was ultimately titled 'Black Sands: High Science as Practical Magic.' And that's another thing—all the chapters got renamed along the way. Just about everything got changed and transformed like an alchemical process, except one thing—the title. *The Sacred Revival*, once it came to my mind, remained as the guiding force throughout. The book's subtitle got tweaked, but the main title stood like a lighthouse over this wayfarer's journey. Perhaps that was why I felt drawn to including the tale of the lighthouse as the epilogue to the book.

So finally, after many months of working on the different chapters, an integral whole of a book emerged. To be truthful, I enjoyed the creative process. It felt like many of the chapters existed as stand-alone pieces and could be read out of the context of the whole book. And although I recommend reading the book from beginning to end as you would normally, I don't feel there would be any great disjuncture if you, the reader, decided to take the chapters in whatever order you felt drawn to. In the end, the final, overall experience would be similar. I guess that's much the same as how the sacred energies work. They are present in each individual part reflecting the integral whole like a hologram.

The sacred revival that is present—and prescient—throughout this book suggests an amalgam of the sacred with the 'matter reality' of our increasingly technological-material cultures.* Yet by technology I also refer to 'technologies of the soul,' and not only those extensions of human society which reach out to connect us with the external world. The sacred, if anything, concerns itself with the communion between interior and exterior realms; it can be called the grand unifier.

This book also takes the view that the 'reality matrix' in which we are embedded, like fish in water, is infused wholly and completely with the phenomenon of consciousness. It is consciousness that is both the background and the foreground of reality, of the sacred nonvisible and a visible reality. The sacred technologies of which the book speaks represent a coming together of the seemingly magical, imaginal realm of the nonvisible with the ever-unfolding realm of our physical—and now also digital—reality. And ultimately, whatever things may *appear* to be, they are all features of humanity searching for its soul and sense of meaning in a world in the process of transformation.

The essential path has no breaks. It is forever consistent, regardless of external form. It is the great game of the alchemists in which we play, and we are learning how to be burned with this secret fire in just the right amount for transmuting us to the next step.

---

* The term matter reality here suggests an emphasis on the material aspect of reality as opposed to the underlying energy field.

This book cannot cover everything within its subject domain. That would require an eternal encyclopedia of Borgesian proportions. Instead, I prefer to consider this book as a series of connecting and communing ripples upon a cosmic, cultural canvas. It is, if nothing else, a conversation between listening minds that, with humble hope, will produce enough fodder for mindful consideration. It is also a conversation about and around the sacred, without giving away any concrete, one-sentence definitions of just what the *sacred* actually is. That's because there is no one sentence or set of words that could define the sacred. It is known not by what it is called, but by the effects of its presence, and its expression in the manifest world. Yet respected thinker Gregory Bateson did try to get close; he said:

> The *sacred* (whatever that means) is surely related (somehow) to the *beautiful* (whatever that means). And if we could say how they are related, we could perhaps say what the words mean. Or perhaps that would never be necessary.[1]

In other words, the sacred cannot easily be pinned down or put specifically into words. Yet it can be perceived and observed by its effects. As is commonly said, do not judge a person by their words, but from their actions. And the sacred impulse calls back to us, whispering *do not do as I say, but do as I do*. The sacred revival is more about *being* and *doing* it, rather than talking about it.

In a similar vein, anthropologist and raconteur Terence McKenna made reference to the 'Archaic Revival,' which he noted had aspects of 'the break-up of patterns that are male dominated and hierarchy based on animal organization, back to the ideal/idea of the vegetation goddess, close to the feminine earth — closer to the gnosis of the vegetable mind, a partnership style of social organization. It suggests the feminizing of culture, an inward search for values, a detoxification of planet and life — to live in symbiosis — a planetary life and evolution.'[2]

There are features, forms, and values here which I see as being part of the present sacred revival. This includes the rise of feminine energies and organization; the interior search and gaze; the healing of life on the planet; an emerging symbiotic ecosystem; and a drive toward planetary consciousness, cohesion, and coherence. One of our greatest needs is for a connection with the transcendent. The old worldview, with its linear, industrial mind, has been crumbling for some time now, whilst the new is struggling to be birthed and articulated. The sacred revival is emerging not in smooth waters but amidst the rapids and vortexes of immense change. Yet nothing is definite, and even this book, as a wayfarer's roadmap, is anything but certain. The French philosopher Voltaire said, 'Doubt is an uncomfortable condition, but certainty is a ridiculous one.' No one, and no thing, goes into the sacred foray with certainty — that's for sure!

In our drive for security and comfort, we often — both individually and collectively — persuade ourselves that we understand when we don't. We are all tied to our cultural expectations and presumptions. Terence McKenna referred to this in a tongue in cheek way when he said: 'To search expectantly for a radio signal from an extraterrestrial source is probably as culture-bound a presumption as to search the galaxy for a good Italian restaurant.'[3] And so we have to let go of some of our expectations and assumptions. It's okay to not understand everything all of the time.

Often in our search for security we end up banishing mystery from our world simply because we are uncomfortable with it. We seek clarity rather than the unknown, and we deny that mystery is a primary force in the cosmos. Our life and its meaning is a mystery most of us care not to unpack. And yet the sacred journey is one of *becoming*, and it requires that we seek this becoming, rather than demanding that we already *be*. After all, nothing exists in a state of completion. Everything is continually in splendid motion. And mystery, with a slice of magic, is part of the process. In the words of philosopher Henryk Skolimowski, 'We are the eyes through which the universe contemplates itself.'[4]

If the gathering of human knowledge is a process — that is, unfolding and developing — then our knowledge of the mysteries of life and cosmos, the divine and the sacred, are also unfolding. As we develop, so does our understanding of the reality which holds us.

There is no isolationism; each is bounded by the other. And like a feedback loop, the more understanding we receive, the more it pushes our perceptions on to ever greater understanding, like water rushing through a vortex and widening it. It is when we pull back out of hesitancy or fear that we stem the onward flow of our growth and realizations.

Another way to look at it is that our reality matrix is already a totally interdependent matrix. It is only our view of it that is fragmented. As in the opening words from Patrick Harpur, 'The world we see is the myth we are in.'[5] Perhaps we do not perceive that we exist as part of a cosmos that is not only participatory but also sensitive. It is sensitive to our presence, participation, and our projections. And the more that science delves into the structure of the cosmos (our reality matrix) the more that structure dissolves from the tangible into the intangible (from matter to energy).

In response to this development, our technologies should manage those relations between the tangible and the intangible to make our world a better place. Technologies are also evolving, since they are extensions of human invention, imagination, and consciousness. As such, they are part of the overall pattern of the sacred tapestry.

The sacred speaks to us through myth, as I explore in the opening chapters. We learn that everything is in flow and flux, even our cycles of time. Myths have sought to connect us with the divine, with the essential.

THE SACRED REVIVAL

When we are distracted, amnesiac, or drowning in a sea of materiality, myths have tried to anchor us. Sometimes we lost those threads that served to guide us to sacred communion.

As a species, we are a collective made up of those who are hypnagogic (falling into sleep) and those who are hypnopompic (waking up from sleep). Amidst this surreal landscape, we are like tribal players juggling with sacred totems and struggling against our dragons. As the ancient mapmakers used to scribe over unknown watery territories, 'Here be dragons.' And from within this shifting territory, we invent our fictions and our superheroes. We play Gnostic games, trancelike and ecstatic, and we dance along the borderlands of the sacred where magic never died.

And now a new moon is rising, reflecting upon the rivers a feminine energy that is coming in to help rid us of our monkey minds. We are being shown that we can dream the world into being and re-soul her body. Our high sciences are like magic, and our technologies can partake in our transcendence. The sacred revival anticipates a new planetary ecosystem coming into arrangement upon the Earth. And the Earth may shake as the sacred resonance comes into our field of view. In the end, it's down to us — are we ready to be the caretakers for a new sacred order?

Let us hope so. It will be worth the ride. . . .

Notes

[1] Quoted in Henryk Skolimowski, *The Participatory Mind: A New Theory of Knowledge and of the Universe* (London: Penguin/Arkana, 1994), 255.

[2] Terence McKenna, *The Archaic Revival* (New York: HarperCollins, 1991), 211.

[3] McKenna, *The Archaic Revival*, 35.

[4] Skolimowski, *The Participatory Mind*, 3.

[5] Patrick Harpur, *The Philosophers' Secret Fire: A History of the Imagination* (Glastonbury: The Squeeze Press, 2009).

1

RE-ENCHANTING THE WORLD: WHERE THERE IS GRACE AND WONDER

The most beautiful experience we can have is the mysterious. It is the fundamental emotion that stands at the cradle of true art and true science. Whoever does not know it and can no longer wonder and stand rapt in awe, is as good as dead, and his eyes are dimmed.
— Albert Einstein, **The World as I See It**

When we look up into the night sky and see the sparkle of stars, we are awed and enchanted. There is grace, there is wonder, and there is the excitement of the unknown. Everything comes alive with possibility. There is an enchanted world out there, and it beckons to us through a communal mystery. And we wish to respond to that call, for underlying all life is the urge for meaning. As human beings we desire, long for, *need* a sense of meaning and purpose in our lives. An enchanted universe serves to entice us with a feeling of belonging. Yet somewhere along the way we lost the sense of communion.

Once, humanity felt a common destiny with its environment, both terrestrial and cosmic, and this encouraged a mode of direct participation. Long ago, the environment experienced by humankind was an immersive space, an inclusive matrix that involved the individual in each moment of their lives. Our ancestors did not stand away from life — they participated directly in its enchantment. This merger between being and environment established a psychic wholeness in humans. Our ancestors were not estranged from the world in the way that modern humanity is. In the last few centuries especially, humankind has increasingly expunged itself out of its own mystery and thrown itself out of the realm of enchantment. Modern scientific, rational consciousness is an alienated consciousness, afraid of its participation. It views the world as an outside observer; a world of objects that move in mechanical motion. This alienated consciousness has substituted the enchantment and mystery with a smear of artificiality. The cosmos of human 'being and belonging' thus became tainted with the contagion of the human mind. Yet this is not how things are, it is only the latest picture of how things *seem to us*. We have been forced to construct our own meanings about a world we have let slip from ourselves. In other words, we have disenchanted ourselves from a living cosmos.

The modern landscape is now more scattered with administration than adventure. The central image of our age has been that of consumerism: the ability of the average person to buy the material goods they require in order to have a decent standard of living. This industrial rhetoric applauded the factory worker's ability to afford the goods they were producing, thus becoming the marketplace itself. Many commentators saw this as the modern individual buying into the system and merging with its insipid ideology. Only recently have some acute observers come to realize that consumerism has morphed into an idiosyncratic crash therapy for people to buy themselves into getting away from the system. The easy acquisition of things has become more about trying to cover up anxiety about the self; a way to placate the anomie and disguise one's ennui. Consumerism is nothing more than the expression of a creeping world-weariness. Our eyes have barely been peering over the brim of our little self worlds.

The inner psychological landscape of many has become infected with this weary contagion. We have now been put on guard to protect our psychic spaces, and also to fend off forces that, intentionally or not, serve to damage and plunge our thoughts into despair. The game playing that has become our lives divorces us from our real sense of self, which then retreats further inward into the deep recesses of our being. Modern life is now rife with false selves parading as authentic entities. This disenchantment became our dominant lens in which we looked out at the world around us — and at the cosmos, too. Everything continued to be one grand accident, a colossal conglomeration of chance and chaos. That was just how life came to be.

The modern history of the West has been about the removal of mystery, mind, and magic from the world around us. Modern Western consciousness defines itself by its very removal from the world 'beyond.' It also unfairly labels all past thinking as not only incorrect, but primitive. That is, we tell ourselves that our understanding of the world has developed and improved in a linear fashion. Thus, all earlier thinking and mental notions were inferior and 'unscientific.' Humankind erroneously positions itself on a belief of linear progress, which is mechanical and immature. Previous worldviews are seen as misguided, illegitimate, and lacking sophistication. And yet we wonder little about how our descendants will look back upon our own current prognosis.

Whether we call our present age the modern or postmodern, the underlying current is the same. So many people seem to be spending their lives not in fear of what may happen to them, but in fear that nothing will happen to them. This malaise has, for many, been turned into an expression of anger and harm, both self-directed and toward others. It is ironic that the very institutions of learning and meaning have recently (in the US predominantly) become the very sites of violence, terror, and meaningless murder. This psychic space, where reality and unreality is in conflict, is a response to our dominant state of consciousness. And yet the consciousness of each age makes its diagnosis, and often unfairly dismisses what came before. For example, we find it extremely difficult to have a grasp upon the consciousness of premodern human society. We can think with our current mental apparatus, yet we are unable to enter into a previous state of consciousness. Hence, the two modes of verification are of different worlds, literally.

The dominant paradigm of human consciousness until recently was largely constructed from the scientific, rational worldview. This is now undergoing a profound transformation as we have entered a period of transition. During such times of change, the impulse for meaning and significance becomes a more prominent and necessary urge. In such moments of sociocultural transformation, when bases of knowledge are revised and our constructions of reality questioned, the need to seek the self grows stronger in the individual.

The rationalist consciousness contained its own built-in limitations, such as its separation from, and disenchantment of, the cosmos. This perspective could only survive for a few centuries — those centuries that were dominated by scientific rationalism and its mechanical universe. The modern scientific paradigm, like the religious paradigm of the seventeenth century, now finds itself unable to be maintained. This is how things unfold; one set of structures, systems, and viewpoints are eventually outmoded and, through necessity (among other factors) get replaced, or rather updated, by a new set. This new set then defines the dominant consciousness for the new era. New values too come to the fore to represent the emergent expression of consciousness.[*]

---

[*] I have discussed these values and the new consciousness in my book *The Phoenix Generation: A New Era of Connection, Compassion, and Consciousness.*

In such transitional times there is urgency, opportunity, and an interior push to reconnect with a sense of meaning, both personal and cosmic. In other words, there is a fundamental need to understand one's self and its place in the larger scheme of things. The instability we encounter in the world around us only convinces us further on the need to find the roots that connect us with a more permanent stream of knowledge and meaning.

IN THE BEGINNING . . .

In the beginning, when conscious, reflective thought arose within humanity, all our mental inquiries were unified into a single stream that was an inherently sacred quest. We longed to know the origins of existence. Philosophy and science were once the same endeavor, and they existed alongside a metaphysical thirst. The human spirit longed to seek beyond the rhythm of the stars and the suns. Our ancestors watched and tracked the cycles of day and night, the great arc of star-sprinkled skies, and the heavenly revolutions. From this they calculated a measurement of time, mathematics, and reason. And with these tools they expanded the mind's reach to traverse the possibilities of life with its whys and wherefores, endlessly searching once again for the original stream of our origins. It is the spirit that seeks and calls out wishing to know and be known, and it is society that clothes the spirit in colored garbs that change with each season's fashions. We've come to wear so many layers around us that we hardly have any remembrance of being naked. And yet the soul of humanity, the soul of the world, has never ceased to be the essential driver that propels us further.

For thousands of years in cultures across the globe—from the ancient Egyptians to Mesoamerica—divination, myth, ritual, and direct intervention with the gods all formed part of the holistic human experience. Dealings with phenomena beyond materiality informed the psychological and spiritual development of human beings. Such mythology constituted a healthy and integral part of human consciousness. Such a premodern consciousness was also one where the ego was kept in check by the presence of powerful transcendental forces that were believed to play a permanent part in human lives. Such transcendental, transhuman powers were perceived as being the real players behind human existence. And such powers were not only acting upon human beings externally, but also formed a part of their interior psyche. As such, the aspects of the individual—their thoughts, feelings, desires, and intentions—were not as strongly developed and manifested as they are today. In such ancient times humankind was not considered apart from such powers, energies, or consequences in the way that the modern individual believes today. This integration within the cosmological order created a natural sense of enchantment.

Yet by the first century CE, the essayist Plutarch was asking, 'Why is it that the gods are no longer speaking to us?' By that time there had been a steep decline in the prestige of the oracles and the divination that was once held so prominent in Greek culture. However, a great majority of people still believed that their lives, both internal and external, were influenced by forces beyond them, those forces which also infused their souls. For millennia the boundaries between inner and outer, and between subjective and objective, had become blurred. One did not know where to place the dividing lines, if indeed there were any. The external world of nature and the inner world of the human psyche were inextricably merged, and both were spiritualized in their own ways. And yet the process of separation was already under way. Rather than being bonded together, the realms became seen as attached through forms of correspondence.

The medieval world — coming after the premodern (or antiquity), and before the modern period — contained within it a stream of consciousness that retained a link to the notion of correspondence. In this context, correspondence implied that things of the world had relations of sympathy between them. Just as women attract men, minerals attract minerals, and oil repels water, so too do sympathies exist between elements of the cosmos and the earth — a Hermetic 'as above, so below' set of relationships. Resemblance and sympathy were known aspects in the medieval mindset, although the church orders worked hard to expel them on charges of heresy.

Thus, many of these practices were termed 'occult' and driven underground.

The modern mind wished to take a step back and to see things in isolation, and not to confuse the relation of things. Those minds that could not agree on the consensus accepted relations were deemed mad or paranoiac. A famous example in literature appears in Cervantes' *Don Quixote* when his character sees the windmills as giants. In his world things 'did not compute,' as we now say. Where there was no consensus programming, the social order saw this as a threat. Or rather, in the medieval world it was a threat to religious order. So the understanding of correspondences eventually went into survival mode and slipped below the external membrane of medieval life. And thus the Middle Ages grew stagnant, as there was little movement in creative vision, myth, and the innovative ideas that propelled cultures forward.

Human consciousness over the centuries has been undergoing a discoupling from the world around it; a distancing that has been referred to as 'disgodding' from nature.* This involves our human nonparticipation with an integral environment, and creating a distance between human beings and everything else. In short, humanity succeeded in taking itself out of the picture by creating a new and different picture of itself. The rejection of the earlier participatory consciousness, often referred to as animism, owes a debt to the emergence

---
*   A phrase from Friedrich Schiller.

of monotheistic religion. It also owes a debt to the rationalistic thinking of Greek thought and philosophy that aimed to push aside instinct in favor of observation and experimentation.

Early monotheistic religion viewed participatory consciousness as sin, while rational Hellenistic thought considered it a pathology of the mind. Both served to expunge it from the human experience and to usher in a discoupled consciousness that has resulted in disenchantment from a vibrant, living cosmos. Yet this did not occur overnight, and fragments of participatory consciousness continued down the ages until it met its end in the Scientific Revolution of seventeenth century.

The Scientific Revolution of seventeenth century Western Europe established a new way of perceiving reality. An important aspect of this shift was a change from quality to quantity and from the why of things to the how. The universe, once seen as alive and having its own purposes, now became inert, a mechanical moratorium of meaningless matter. Nature became a thing to be probed and controlled, stepped back from and observed, rather than as something to merge and participate with. Being at home in the cosmos became relegated to romantic fantasies, as purposive manipulation of the environment took its place on the human playing field. The conscious commodity management of the world replaced the enchanted wonder of a magical life. Humanity had made a complete turnabout from participant (early humankind), to passive observers (religious revolution), to material manipulators (Scientific Revolution). The ideas of the Scientific Revolution were put fully into play during the industrial revolutions.

The collapse of the feudal economy and the rise of capitalism as a major force profoundly altered social relations in modern Europe and created a social context for the embrace of the Scientific Revolution. Quantification and control would not have had its place in a medieval world, yet was ideally suited to these times; hence, its emergence. Modern science is ideally suited to a world of capital accumulation. It seems that both ideologies share a similar mental framework: an industrial mentality and worldview.

The medieval worldview had its own sense of completeness, where divine principle ordered the movement, positions, and purpose of all life in the heavens, as above and below. The world thus became endowed with meaning, albeit its own interpretation of meaning. The notion of a God was pivotal at this time, only to be squeezed out later by the bastion of science. The individual in medieval times had meaning allotted to them, regardless of it being beneficial or not to their social welfare. The individual of the scientific, rationalist era had to search through the newly declared inert environment to seek their own sense of significance. It was a totally different world. The scientific mind could give us facts and data, but it fell short in providing values.

A psychological shift also occurred that dramatically affected the individual. The closed medieval world, with its feudal structure, country folk, religious order, and close networks, provided a psychologically safe and secure environment. The advent of the rationalist era changed all this when it threw the individual mind into a brutal world of merciless mechanism, management, and meaningless industrial, urban landscapes. The individual of the new modern Europe lost their purposeful footing in the race for nationalist expansion in an uncaring universe.

Nationalist expansion also meant naval expansion, as the old world opened up to the new. Science helped in creating instruments and methods for naval navigation, as well as for colonial conquest. Expansion of territory and consciousness went hand in hand, and the closed medieval European world was left behind in the enviable pursuit of progress. Long-distance trading spurred on the rise of a revolution in commerce that quashed local artisan and barter trade. The mercantile class gradually replaced the guild master and journeyman, personal trade relationships broke down, and credit systems arose to fill the demand. Despite this changeover being written within only a few sentences, on the historical stage it was a tremendous shift that psychologically altered the mentality, perception, and worldview of Europeans.

The ecumenical order of the medieval world was replaced by the new economic order. The logic and rationality of this was that when salvation and pardon could be bought by money, those with money had salvation. Economy became the divine goal for the new era of progress. Financial calculation became the new road to comprehending the once creative cosmos. Rational calculation was as amenable to the cosmos, to nature, as it was to the financial economy. A new completeness had been found that sat comfortably within the scientific, rational, industrial worldview. A new modern Europe was being constructed that viewed progress separate from the meaning and metaphysical significance of the individual. With the cosmos as something within concrete laws, the latest pioneers of humankind could continue unabated with their goals of conquest and competition. A new type of consciousness had seated itself at the forefront of human social development.

The late seventeenth and early eighteenth centuries did their best to discard, disprove, and remove the inner psychic landscape of human beings, the inner reality, as it did not adhere to the incoming programs of capitalist commerce and industrial mechanization, expansion, and management.

Despite the seemingly outward appearance of stability, human civilization on the whole has been in a state of instability and crisis for several centuries. The modern schismatic consciousness that has been embraced as being normal has led us to the present state of world volatility. It is not about thinking straight, as we have been led to believe, but rather about thinking relational. The Cartesian-Newtonian paradigm, which split the world into parts and mechanized their relations, ruptured the necessary harmony between all things. Such a state of affairs is now nothing more than antiquated.

By the time we look back on this from a new phase of human civilization historians will see the Cartesian-Newtonian paradigm as a relic. It will be viewed as a curiosity of mind that created rapid industrial expansion and scientific knowledge, yet failed to bring real progress upon the essence of human beings. Its spurt, which lasted several centuries, may be likened to a primitive rocket booster that propels a ship into orbit only to be spent and cast off, to fry up and dissolve as it falls back down to earth. The last few centuries were a single evolutionary episode that ran its course. In anthropological terms, it was a mere blink of an eye. And in that blink, humanity brought itself to the brink of collapse. Yet at the very last step, it seems it has pulled itself back onto the path as a new evolutionary epoch pushes through with disruptive labor into planetary birth.

We are in the midst of that birthing transition now, as the collective mind of humankind seeks solace in a new era of communion with an enchanted, sacred cosmos. We are not so much in a new age, but rather in a new gnosis, where so many revolutionary—or rather evolutionary—strands of the enlightening fabric are weaving together to form a new tapestry. We have the discoveries of new science—of the quantum world in physics and biology—mingling with new technologies of the outer and the inner world. We have various mystical traditions mingling through mixed cultures and pushing ancient knowledge into the mainstream; and the inner landscape of humanity is being increasingly traversed and mapped through exploratory and psychic tools. The digital, virtual words are augmenting our sense of material reality, and the deep cosmos is exploding into revelation and being revealed.

The great sacred mirror of the human self is reflecting back to us every known atom that ever sprang out of the creative matrix of existence. It is the age of momentum, acceleration, exposure, disclosure, invention, innovation, exploration, and Gnostic understanding as never before on such a widespread scale. It is nothing short of a profound planetary movement—a bright light of great awe and epiphany. It is a truly miraculous age to be witness to what is unfolding. We are now aiming toward a new stage of human fusion on a planetary level. Humanity longs for unification, for an integral empathy of relations and communion. The medieval mind referred to this as a form of *sympathy*, of *correspondences*, between things; a merging between object and subject where distinctions become their attraction. This is the sacred reality that needs to be reinstalled into the collective consciousness of humankind. And it has been there all along, swimming around in our mythic archetypes below the thin surface crust of the conscious mind. Now it is awakening, and the new era emerging will have no alternative but to encourage, embrace, and celebrate this sacred revival of an enchanted cosmos.

And yet arriving at the point where we are now has been a historical roller coaster of ups and downs on the physical level, too. The notion of a sacred revival suggests that humanity has been here before, as if we have completed another lap upon the ascending spiral. While this chapter has introduced us to the psychological fluctuations in human civilization, the next chapter will look at some of the twists and turns upon the historical route.

2

COMING AROUND AGAIN: THE FLOWS AND FLUXES OF HISTORY

We shall not cease from exploration
And the end of all our exploring
Will be to arrive where we started
And know the place for the first time.
– T. S. Eliot, **'Little Gidding'**

The most wonderful aspect of life still seems to me that some coarse and crude intervention and even blatant violation can become the occasion for establishing a new order within us.
– Rainer Maria Rilke, Letters on Life

Everything comes around again. It seems that the cosmos and all life within it do not do straight lines. The fall from one high type of human culture, civilization, or era into a period of barbarism appears to be a regular feature in the flow and flux of planetary life. Epochs of high spiritual exploration and understanding have often plunged into periods of obscurantism and materialism. These patterns are played out upon the chessboard of history, as well as in our mythic narratives. What we take for human history is more often than not a fragmented collage of collective amnesia, artificially reconstructed into a comprehensible sense of linear progress.

The truth of such passages of time may instead be closer to a far grander historical pattern that moves in vast cycles of growth and decline. As an example, we may take the speculative view supplied by Brian Aldiss's science fiction series, the Helliconia trilogy. In this work the planet Helliconia moves through a much larger time cycle in which one of its years, called The Great Year, is equivalent to some 2,500 Earth years. Each book in the trilogy follows the rise and fall of civilization through each season (spring, summer, winter). By the end of summer, human-type civilization upon the planet has developed to a level similar to that of advanced European Renaissance, only to inevitably regress once again when the centuries-long winter arrives. The trilogy also suggests that some elements of human society are able to preserve knowledge during the winter dark ages that can be used in the coming season or cycle to once again develop a scientific, industrial civilization.
In a similar manner, we may infer that our very own civilization is in the early throes of its spring, casting off the old systems that helped it achieve passage through the intervening 'winter' centuries. As Indian sage Sri Aurobindo noted:

> Emerging from the periods of eclipse and the nights of ignorance which overtake humanity, we assume always that we are instituting new knowledge. In reality, we are continually rediscovering the knowledge and repeating the achievement of the ages that have gone before us.[1]

Rediscovery may be the appropriate term for framing how the sacred is due for its resurgence into the seemingly fragmented crux of our postmodern life. Being in the midst of a revival denotes the continuation of a tradition and not its beginnings. It may be of use to us then to take a further peek into this notion of grand historical cycles.

Ancient myths and stories from around the world speak of the flow and flux of epochs and civilizations as part of a grand cosmic cycle of growth and decay. Archaeological records are forever being updated to reveal new evidence of the decline and collapse of civilizations throughout the ancient world. This trend in the decline of civilizations was recently (relatively speaking) seen in the early Middle Ages in which there was a time of contraction where long-distance travel and trade almost ceased overnight. This period of renewed tribalism, warlords, and serfdom is commonly referred to as the Dark Ages, circa 500 CE. Then, almost a thousand years later, as if on cue, the wheel began to turn again and a new creative impulse emerged in the knowledge, scientific discovery, and artistic expression that was the Renaissance period. Many ancient myths and teachings state that there is a pattern to this ebb and flow that delineates the fall away from knowledge into base materialism and brutality. One of the most explicit teachings on this cyclic trend is in the Hindu Yugas.

In Hindu philosophy the Yugas refer to a grand epoch that is divided into four ages: the Satya Yuga (Golden Age), Treta Yuga (Silver Age), Dwapara Yuga (Bronze Age), and Kali Yuga (Iron Age). Hindu cosmology tells us that the universe is created and destroyed each full day of Brahma (lasting up to eight billion of our years). In this time the cycles of creation and destruction repeat like passing seasons, shifting from periods of greater growth (spring) to times of decline and hibernation (winter). In this analogy both human civilization and consciousness, like the seasons on Earth, go through changes. It is written that the grand Yuga cycles affect the phases of life on the planet and also the capacities of the human psyche. A complete Yuga cycle passes from a high period of growth (Golden Age) to a period of decline (Dark Age) and back again. However, the exact dating and timing of the Yuga cycles has attracted great controversy and disagreement. According to the Laws of Manu, one of the earliest known texts describing the Yugas, the length is:

- Satya Yuga: 4,800 years
- Treta Yuga: 3,600 years
- Dwapara Yuga: 2,400 years
- Kali Yuga: 1,200 years

This dating gives a total of 12,000 years to complete one arc of the cycle (declining from the Golden Age to the Iron Age). In order to complete one full cycle (back from the Iron Age to the Golden Age), another 12,000 years is required, making a grand total of 24,000 years. This figure is relatively close to the 26,000 years of the precession of the equinoxes as understood by modern science. It may be likely that the ancient astronomers were attempting to correlate the Yuga cycle with the Great Year as they had calculated the rate of the Earth's precession slightly differently, to 50" yearly. With their calculation, the Great Year would have been roughly 24,000 years, in line with their Yuga cycle dating. Modern science, however, has more recently calculated the rate of precession to be 50.1" yearly (or 1°0" in 72 years) making it not 24,000, but 25,920 years for the vernal equinox to make one whole circle of the zodiac. So in the end, it appears that there is a strong correlation between the cyclic precession of the equinoxes and the Hindu Yugas.

There is still some debate as to the correct duration of the Yugas. More recent, and popular, interpretations measure the years in terms of the demigods (one year of the demigods is equal to 360 human years), making the Yugas much longer. For example, the 4,800 years of the Satya Yuga would now be 4,800 x 360, which equals 1,728,000 years. Yet the highly respected nineteenth and twentieth century Indian yogi Swami Sri Yukteswar Giri (teacher of Paramahansa Yogananda) agrees with the shorter duration that correlates with the earliest known texts of the Laws of Manu. Still, the question remains: which Yuga cycle are we currently in? The obvious answer might be to say that we are in the Kali Yuga, the Iron Age, to which many commentators readily concur. However, this may not be the case. Again, it is a matter of number crunching to find the exact dating. In his book *The Holy Science*, Sri Yukteswar wrote that during the later years of the Dwapara era (about 700 BCE):

> Maharaja Yudhisthira, noticing the appearance of the dark Kali Yuga, made over his throne to his grandson [and] . . . together with all of his wise men . . . retired to the Himalaya Mountains. . . .Thus there was none in the court . . . who could understand the principle of correctly accounting the ages of the several Yugas.[2]

Sri Yukteswar tells us that at the court of Yudhisthira's grandson there was no one who correctly understood the coming of the Kali Yuga, so they kept adding years to the Dwapara date. Therefore, when the last year of the 2,400 year period of Dwapara Yuga passed away, and the first year of the 1,200 year Kali Yuga Dark Age had arrived, the latter was numbered as the year 2401 instead of year 1 of Kali Yuga. In 498 CE, when the 1,200 year period of Kali Yuga of the descending arc had been completed and the first year of Kali Yuga of the ascending arc begun, the latter was designated in the Hindu almanacs as the year 3601 instead of year 1 of Kali Yuga of the ascending arc.[3]

With this new understanding of the dating of the Yuga ages, the present full cycle has been calculated as:

- Satya Yuga (Golden Age of humanity): 11,502 to 6702 BCE
- Treta Yuga (Silver Age, descending arc): 6702 to 3102 BCE
- Dwapara Yuga (Bronze Age, descending arc): 3102 to 702 BCE
- Kali Yuga (Iron Age, descending arc): 702 BCE to 498 CE (the peak of the early Middle Ages to the Dark Ages, after the fall of Rome)
- Kali Yuga (Iron Age, ascending arc): 498 to 1698 CE
- Dwapara Yuga (Bronze Age, ascending arc): 1698 to 4098 CE
- Treta Yuga (Silver Age, ascending arc): 4098 to 7698 CE
- Satya Yuga (next Golden Age): to commence in 7698 CE

In terms of attributes, the Yugas generally highlight the rise and fall of great civilizations as well as the ebb and flow in the morality, ethics, and the quality of consciousness in humankind. During the descending arc, not only do civilizations become more materially based, but there is also a loss of truth, wisdom, sincerity, and integrity, as if saintliness turns into decadence. According to Sri Yukteswar, in the period of Satya Yuga, the Golden Age, humanity comprehends the source of universal divinity and how the universe is sustained, has complete wisdom, oneness, purity, and intelligence, and works with the finest energies of the cosmos. In Treta

Yuga, the Silver Age, humanity has lost its peak of oneness, yet still works with an extensive knowledge and power over universal energies (such as magnetism) and cosmic forces, and constructs harmonious and peaceful cities and civilizations. In Dwapara Yuga, the Bronze Age, humanity retains a comprehension of some of the finer forces and more subtle energies of the cosmos and various forces of attraction and repulsion, and understands that all matter, all atomic form, is nothing other than the manifestation of energy and vibratory forces. Finally, in Kali Yuga, the Iron Age, humankind's knowledge and power is restricted to the world of gross matter, and is focused primarily upon material concerns.

Sri Yukteswar also tells us that each ascending age enhances humanity's mental faculties and clarity of understanding, which includes knowledge of the finer forces at work within the cosmos. This begins with a rudimentary understanding of electrical forces. Yukteswar writes:

> About 1600, William Gilbert discovered magnetic forces and observed the presence of electricity in all material substances. In 1609 Kepler discovered important laws of astronomy, and Galileo produced a telescope. In 1621 Drebbel of Holland invented the microscope. About 1670 Newton discovered the law of gravitation. In 1700 Thomas Savery made use of a steam engine in raising water. Twenty years later Stephen Gray discovered the action of electricity on the human body.[4]

As we are currently in the early decades of the twenty-first century, according to Sri Yukteswar (who wrote his book in 1894), we are now several centuries into the ascending arc of Dwapara Yuga (which began in 1698). Hence, if Sri Yukteswar's timeline is correct, we should now be discovering that energy underlies matter, as well as developing sciences that work with even finer molecular and electrical forces. Indeed, the advent of quantum mechanics in the early part of the twentieth century has led to a revolution in how we understand universal forces, and there have been rapid advancements in the quantum sciences (biology, computing, etc.). We are also now developing our new sciences referred to collectively as NBIC—nanotechnology, biotechnology, information technology, and cognitive science—as if right on cue. However, a question that should be asked now is, are the Yugas really a serious way of understanding human history and of framing our social, scientific, and psychic development?

Despite the absence of conventional data on the cyclic nature of history, there are clues, allegories, signs, and revelations in various diverse sacred scriptures. These include the Bible, the Vedas of the Hindus, the Egyptians' Book of Thoth, the Avesta of Zoroaster, the Kabbalistic Zohar of the Hebrews, the Völuspá of the ancient Scandinavians, the Popol Vuh of the ancient Mayans, the Tanjur of the Tibetans, and the mystical Hymns of Orpheus. In Ecclesiastes, one of the Wisdom

Books in the Old Testament attributed to Solomon it is written:

> The thing that hath been, it is that which shall be; and that which is done is that which shall be done; and there is no new thing under the sun.
>
> Is there anything whereof it may be said, see, this is new? It hath been already of old time, which was before us.
>
> There is no remembrance of former things; neither shall there be any remembrance of things that are to come with those that shall come after. (Ecclesiastes 1:9–11)

Also Plato, in a well-known extract, reveals in his *Timaeus* that the Egyptians held oral records of past bygone civilizations:

> Thereupon one of the priests, who was of a very great age, said . . . 'You Hellenes are never anything but children, and there is not an old man among you . . . there is no old opinion handed down among you by ancient tradition, nor any science which is hoary with age. And I will tell you why. There have been, and will be again, many destructions of mankind arising out of many causes; the greatest have been brought about by the agencies of fire and water . . . and so you have to begin all over again like children, and know nothing of what happened in ancient times, either among us or among yourselves.'[5]

Mainstream archaeological research may reject the cyclic theory of civilizations, yet as a relatively young science, it has in effect only scraped the surface of human history. Much knowledge still lies untouched and, literally speaking, under the ground. It is likely that many unknown ancient civilizations also lie inaccessible under the oceans of the world, sunken and hidden through millennia of geophysical upheaval and cataclysms. Examples include the recent discovery of a civilization five thousand years older than the Indus Valley culture, found in the Gulf of Khambhat (formerly known as the Gulf of Cambay) in the Arabian Sea off the west coast of India. There are also the underwater structures, including a pyramid, wide terraces, and ramps and steps, that have been found in Japanese waters off the island of Yonaguni near Okinawa. There have been similar recent discoveries that have filled books of what is now termed 'alternative history,' and which is largely shunned and ridiculed by mainstream traditional scholars.

All knowledge, and this applies especially to academic study, is in a constant state of update and renewal; it is never a finished product. No doubt then, our consensus knowledge on the rise and fall of past civilizations is also lacking. Current mainstream theories prefer to believe that a primitive humanity emerged from a Paleolithic Age and entered a Neolithic or New Stone Age of rudimentary agriculture and into the first faint beginnings of human culture about 15,000 BCE. In other words, the history of human civilization is linear: a straight path from hunter-gatherers to the industrialists of today. Yet as Sri Aurobindo says, 'The savage is perhaps not so much the first forefather of civilised man as the degenerate descendent of a previous civilisation. . . . Barbarism is an intermediate sleep, not an original darkness.'[6] The truth of the matter is more likely to be that history 'follows a circular (rather, a spiral) course, with upward and downward half-circles which blend into each other as naturally and inevitably as day follows night, and season succeeds season. Scholars grant that a cycle of growth and decadence is evident in the history of all past empires and cultures, but they have not yet perceived that the trend of civilization as a whole follows a similar cycle.'[7]

In the understanding of Yuga cycles outlined here, the descending arc of the cycle will witness the gradual loss of immense knowledge and heritage of the previous great epochs. This loss will be scattered and strewn into fragments through descending millennia, their remnants and traces considered as anomalies, until the known historical achievements of humankind are nothing other than relics during the final arc of descent. It could well be that past records and traces of once-great civilizations have vanished so completely that modern scholars will never admit the possibility of their ever existing.

The remnants of past civilizations that we do know something of cannot be considered primitive just because they came before us. This is especially so when even today architects say they cannot replicate the exact precision of the building of the Egyptian pyramids — even with the most modern technology. Let us consider also the remnants found at different places around the world: the grandiose Hindu ruins of Ellora in the Deccan, the Mayan Chichen Itza in Yucatan, and the grand ruins of Copán in Honduras, among many others. The cyclic theory of ascent and descent begins to make more sense when we consider that the lowest point of the cycle was said to have been reached in 498 CE, at exactly the same time that much of the world was plunged into the near-barbarism that accompanied the fall of the Roman Empire and the breakup of western lands into tribal regions. This theory of cycles in human civilization accounts for the lack of continuity in the progress of humankind. It also provides a pattern for why it appears that sociocultural evolution seems to abound in start-stop spurts rather than to progress in a clear, developmental, linear fashion. Finally, it may provide a context in which to understand the creative peaks and declines in the realization and expression in human consciousness. If this is so, then it gives greater credibility to the existence of a stream of sacred wisdom that would have been crucial in preserving and maintaining a lineage of transmission during such sociocultural flux. And if this is the case, then this cyclic dating also tells us we are on the upswing in the enhancement of our mental, psychic, and spiritual faculties.

OUR CURRENT RESURGENCE

The great revival of learning in Europe can be said to have begun in the fifteenth century with the introduction of the printing press and paper manufacturing (paper was first brought to Europe from China by the Arabs). Europe was once again introduced to the old classical cultures; the thought of ancient Greece and Rome, and of Babylon and Egypt. Certain European classical literature, including the writings of Dante, Chaucer, and later Shakespeare and Goethe, is now recognized as having been greatly influenced by Arabic sources. The European Renaissance was a flowering of thought and culture which occurred at the crux of the ascending arc of the next Yuga, the Dwapara Yuga.

The Dwapara Yuga, or the Bronze Age, of the ascending arc began, according to our time references, in 1698. In the past four centuries of Dwapara Yuga the world has, by and large, made greater strides forward in knowledge and discovery than in all the twenty-four centuries (comprising two Kali Yugas) that have preceded the modern period. Great industrial and technological discoveries and inventions have transformed the world over the last few centuries. As human civilization increasingly leaves the Iron Age behind, we notice a gradual parallel move away from the heavier structural materials of iron and steel towards the use of lighter and finer materials.

The Industrial Revolution peaked in the use of these heavier technologies that served to open up expansion in transportation and urban growth. The Dwapara Age that began in 1698 is marked by an understanding of what Sri Yukteswar termed 'fine matter forces.' In other words, advances in the understanding and use of forces that are more subtle and less physical, such as electrical, and then later molecular and atomic forces. As humanity progresses along this ascending cycle, it is said we are set to increase our understanding of the forces and energies of the universe, leading to many new discoveries. Indeed, we are already well into the age of electricity and its finer, more ethereal qualities as evidenced by the emergence of global communications, the Internet, and the fast-developing digital age. The rapid advancement of new forms and modes of technology (magic made flesh) will be returned to later in the book. Yet this pattern is indicative of movement through the ascending arc that shifts us away from heavier materials and energies toward more subtle energies that may comprise magnetic, quantum, or even the infamous 'free energy' sources. This then raises the question of how such exposure to new energy relations will impact human consciousness.

Part of the argument regarding the sacred revival is that human consciousness is being prepared for a period of ascending awareness. I now turn to another stream of information in this regard — transpersonal psychology. Christopher Bache, an educator in transpersonal psychology, initiated a series of sessions in an altered state of consciousness. From these sessions, involving himself, Bache unexpectedly received a 'download' of amazing visions. In these visions he witnessed a global system collapse, followed by the gradual crystallization of a new planetary culture. Bache speaks of a social awakening that is coming, a time when we will shift from the 'atomized cells of our historical past' toward a more integrative and inclusive communion. Everything we are currently undergoing, in our personal lives and on a global level, he says, is paving the way for this future. What follows are some short sample extracts taken from the series of visions that Bache experienced:

> Out of the seething desires of history, out of the violent conflicts and of the scheming of individuals and nations, there was now driving forward a new awareness in human consciousness. Its birth in us no less difficult or violent than the birth of a new continent through volcanic upheaval.
>
> What is emerging is a consciousness of unprecedented proportions, the entire human species integrated into a unified field of awareness. The species reconnected with its fundamental nature. Our thoughts tuned to Source Consciousness. Having moved beyond linear time into 'Deep Time,' I experienced this both as a projected destiny and also as a realised actuality. It was simultaneously something to be accomplished and something already accomplished.

COMING AROUND AGAIN

> I saw humanity climbing out of a valley and just ahead, on the other side of the mountain peak and beyond our present sight, was a brilliant, sun-drenched world that was about to break over us. The time frame was enormous. After millions of years of struggle and ascent, we were poised on the brink of a sunrise that would forever change the conditions of life on this planet. All current structures would quickly become irrelevant. All truths would quickly be rendered passé. Truly a new epoch was dawning. The lives of everyone living on the edge of this pivotal time in history had been helping to bring about this global shift.
>
> I repeatedly saw extended webs of energy suddenly contract and explode in brilliant flashes. In the past these flashes had not endured long and had been swallowed by the inertia of the collective unconscious of our species. Now, however, the flashes were beginning to hold their own. Not only were they not dissolving, but they were beginning to connect with other flashes occurring around the planet.[8]

In the final extract we read that Bache experienced various flashes of awakening consciousness around the planet that were beginning to stay on and connect. This image, or interior vision, suggests a permanence of heightened consciousness beginning to manifest. In his work in transpersonal states of consciousness, Bache also gained the understanding that humanity is nearing an era whereby physical experience will be more influenced through the power of 'coherent consciousness' (Bache's term). This concept of coherent consciousness will be discussed in greater depth later in chapter seventeen.

It is significant to say at this point in our sacred story that the historical indications of Swami Sri Yukteswar, and the transpersonal visions of Christopher Bache, are just two examples, from many others, which suggest we are moving through a major social, psychological, and spiritual shift as a species. I propose that the inner psyche of humanity has already been tossed into the tumbler that precipitates major cleansing and change—and this is all part and parcel of the mystery and meaning in our resurging sacred revival. But what, I wonder, do our myths have to say about all this? Perhaps in the next chapter we may find out.

Notes

[1] Quoted in Georges van Vrekhem, *Patterns of the Present: From the Perspective of Sri Aurobindo and The Mother* (Charleston: Van Vrekhem, 2012/2002), 18.

[2] Swami Sri Yukteswar, *The Holy Science* (Los Angeles, CA: Self-Realization Fellowship, 1894/1990).

[3] Laurie Pratt, 'Astrological World Cycles,' *East West Magazine*, 1932.

[4] Yukteswar, *The Holy Science*, 14.

[5] Plato, *Timaeus and Critias* (London: Penguin, 2008).

[6] Quoted in Vrekhem, *Patterns of the Present*, 22.

[7] Pratt, 'Astrological World Cycles.'

[8] Christopher Bache, *Dark Night, Early Dawn* (New York: Suny, 2000).

3

SEEKING OUR MYTHOLOGIES: WHERE DID ALL THE GODS GO?

And so, in mythological terms, what is to happen now? All of our old gods are dead, and the new have not yet been born.
—Joseph Campbell, *The Inner Reaches of Outer Space*

Stories emphasize the operations of divine immanence in the world.
—Jonathan Black, *The Sacred History*

In the beginning, there were many myths of creation. Many of the great spiritual traditions told of how the material world came into being out of a nameless domain. Some traditions have spoken of the 'cosmic egg' from which form emerged; or, as in the Old Testament, out of the dark and formless deep where the spirit of God moved:

> In the beginning God created the heaven and the earth; and the earth was without form, and void; and darkness [was] upon the face of the deep. And the Spirit of God moved upon the face of the waters. (Genesis 1:1-1:2)

The Hindu spiritual traditions of India speak of an underlying reality that is Brahman—a reality that is eternal and eternally unchanging. The world of space and time that we are familiar with is known as *lila*, which describes our physical world as the playground of unceasing creative play within Brahman. In terms of this cosmology, humanity is indeed at play in the fields of the Lord. The ancient Hindu Vedic rishis told that the essence of all things in the material world belonged to *Akasha*. A Sanskrit term, Akasha refers to the fifth element of the cosmos, beyond air (*vata*), fire (*agni*), water (*jal*), and earth (*prithvi*). The concept of Akasha is similar to the later Western notions of *aether* – a space field that contains all the elements within itself. In the late sixteenth century BCE Pythagoras spoke of the 'aether' as the fifth element of the world, in addition to earth, air, fire, and water. In more modern terminology we see similarities with the notion of the underlying quantum vacuum (or plenum) that is described as the energetic sea of the cosmos from which matter reality manifests. Whether you call it the Akasha, aether, or quantum matrix, this is the cosmic energy domain from which everything has emerged, and into which everything will ultimately return.

Western streams of philosophic thought also speak of a domain beyond space and time. According to Plato there was a realm of Forms or Ideas, a domain of pure Forms, beyond our space and time, and that our material world is only an image or copy of this real, pure world beyond. This pure realm was also spoken of by other Hellenic philosophers. Pythagoras referred to it as *Kosmos*, and Plotinus as 'the One.'

Perhaps the most famous illustration of Plato's thinking is his allegory of the Cave. In this allegory Plato describes a group of people who have lived all their lives chained up and facing the wall of a cave. All they can see is the blank cave wall that lies in front of them. The opening of the cave is behind them, and the light that enters casts shadows on the far wall of the cave. Upon this wall, day after day, the chained people watch shadows move across, since they cannot turn around and see the 'real' objects that pass behind them. Thus, they view these shadows as their reality and ascribe forms, reason, and life to them. This is the illusion, the shadows from beyond, that we ascribe as our reality and give meaning to.

Similarly, the Chinese sage Laozi spoke of all things originating in the Tao as the unseen root of all material things. The Tao is both the originator (the source) of all things, and the destination to which all things eventually return. It is the unobservable and nameless no-space, no-time, no-form essence that our words fail. Are these non-spaces the realms where our gods dwell?

Our myths may be the only threads that connect us with such realms; they are the narratives that remain in the earthly domain to help jolt our memories. In his theory of anamnesis, Plato says humanity possesses knowledge of its past, only that we have forgotten this knowledge and so we need to rediscover the knowledge within us. Plato wrote that humanity could only know the 'real world' in the form of memories. That is, human thought was really a form of recollection, and that humankind generally existed within a state of collective amnesia, having only fragments of recollection as reference points for reality.

Plato was suggesting that humanity had lost — or fallen — from an earlier state of heightened awareness and now had only traces of this memory in their collective psyche as a reminder. In ancient Greek, truth is called *aletheia*, which means 'not forgetting.' In Greek mythology, before the human soul incarnates into this world, it drinks from Lethe, the river of forgetfulness and one of the five rivers of the underworld, so that it cannot remember its divine origins. Similarly, there is a Jewish legend that speaks of how we are struck on the mouth by an angel before birth so that we cannot speak of our pre-birth divine origins.

Humanity is being told through these and other related myths that we need to learn how to remember, that truth is recollection, not cognition. We arrive in this earthly reality full of cosmic glory — except that we lack the key, the crucial guide, to unlock our memories and unleash the flood of knowing. When we come across the scattered symbols and signs of truth, we inherently intuit and sense deep down some great significance. Yet our minds are incapable of grasping the intangibleness of this hidden mystery. And that is how our lives play out, as we slip as souls within a playground of signs that are invested with ultimate meaning. We need to find Ariadne's thread to help us through this labyrinth that we find ourselves in, and to remember that we have our origins in the primary imagination. Our lives are not only unique creations, they are acts of re-creation. They are attempts at entering once again into a lost remembrance which lies so far and yet so close to us. The thirteenth century Persian poet Jalāl ad-Dīn Rūmī, in a well-known aphorism, said: 'The Truth is closer to us than our own jugular vein.' And yet in vain do we search, as if we have fallen away from true remembrance.

MYTHS LOST AND REGAINED

One of humanity's most enduring mythic narratives is what is commonly referred to as *the Fall*. What this generally suggests is a break with, or fall away from, another state. This is often interpreted as a break away from a heightened state of connection and awareness, or a disconnection from the living truth. This implies that collective images and myths reappear in our minds, in our histories, as grand archetypes that serve as signifiers to assist humanity in its recollection of lost memories. Touching upon this, Carl Gustav Jung wrote:

> Our psyche is set up in accord with the structure of the universe, and what happens in the macrocosm likewise happens in the infinitesimal and most subjective reaches of the psyche.[1]

Here, Jung is highlighting the distinct correspondence between the human psyche and its synchronization with the grander universe of which we are a part. This emphasizes the notion of the participatory mind, a concept that was known, if not articulated, among our premodern ancestors.

It has been suggested by various psychologists that humanity resonates closely with the notion of the Fall from Paradise because we carry within our collective consciousness vestiges of a remembrance. That is, we have a deep intuitive sense that we once belonged to something higher, to which we may one day return. It seems that within our interior selves lies the hope of returning to something once lost—a Paradise Lost, or some sacred state of communion. This idea has been expressed in allegorical form in many tales, such as in this one called 'The Precious Jewel,' which has been adapted from Eastern sources:

> In a remote realm of perfection, there was a just monarch who had a wife and a wonderful son and daughter. They all lived together in happiness. One day the father called his children before him and said: 'The time has come, as it does for all. You are to go down, an infinite distance, to another land. You shall seek and find and bring back a precious Jewel.' The travellers were conducted in disguise to a strange land, whose inhabitants almost all lived a dark existence. Such was the effect of this place that the two lost touch with each other, wandering as if asleep. From time to time they saw phantoms, similitudes of their country and

of the Jewel, but such was their condition that these things only increased the depth of their reveries, which they now began to take as reality. When news of his children's plight reached the king, he sent word by a trusted servant, a wise man: 'Remember your mission, awaken from your dream, and remain together.' With this message they roused themselves, and with the help of their rescuing guide they dared the monstrous perils which surrounded the Jewel, and by its magic aid returned to their realm of light, there to remain in increased happiness for evermore.[2]

This parable reveals how a latent message lays hidden deep within us, and acts as a chord of remembrance, keeping us connected with something essential yet forgotten.

Mythologists Joseph Campbell and Mircea Eliade have both shown that one story in particular threads its way through nearly all traditions and myths — the story of a lost idyllic golden age. This mythical narrative tells of the hero's journey to restore the world to its former glory. It is frequently a tale of loss and represents the need for heroic restoration. It is also a journey to reconnect ourselves with a sense of the sacred; to restore the bond with a cosmos that enfolds humanity within a universal sense of meaning, where the human psyche merges into the significant whole.

Many myths recovered from the past, and from indigenous tribes, reveal a worldview of our ancients that accepted all things as part of a living, conscious, and sacred cosmos. Within this cosmological view, all life was viewed as connected with an animating energy that was interwoven throughout. As mythological researcher Richard Heinberg writes:

> I feel compelled toward the view that our cultural memories of a Golden Age of harmony are the residue of a once-universal understanding of the spiritual dimension of human consciousness, and are at the same time memories of how contact with that dimension has been almost completely severed.[3]

The contact may appear almost severed, yet traces of it have remained in various traditions, some more obscure than others. This once bygone state that the stories and myths refer to as the Golden Age, or 'paradise,' can also be regarded as a metaphor for an evolved state of consciousness as well as a highly evolved state of civilization. Humankind's state is that of having fallen into the grip of gross matter, and of having left behind a finer awareness of subtle energies. We have, as all major spiritual traditions commonly state, entered into a realm of separation from a divine or sacred source.

Mircea Eliade, in his *The Sacred and the Profane,* writes that every historical culture regarded the human condition as being under a temporary spell of unnatural limitation and separateness. Also, that our world now contains symbols and signs that serve to jolt human consciousness into some degree of reawakened awareness and remembrance, such as in the tale of the Precious Jewel told above. Eliade reminds us that in so-called 'primitive' societies the act of understanding the symbol can help one succeed in 'living the universal.' Similarly, mythologist Joseph Campbell describes how the aim of ancient spiritual practices, tribal myths, and shamanic teachings was to assist in recovering a lost mode of awareness.

It is easy to conclude that the myth of paradise (or of a Golden Age) represents an innate and universal longing, deep within humanity, for a return to a state of tranquility from which we have become separated. Metaphorically, it may indicate that the inner being of each human, when in its natural and essential state, is in balance and harmony. Perhaps there have been historical ages in which human beings shared a state of oneness or union with all life and with their environment, and that this peak of civilization was indeed lost. The Hopi legend of the 'First People' talks of a time in the ancient past when people 'felt as one and understood one another without talking,' which perhaps suggests a form of collective communion. This legend describes a time when humans on the planet manifested a form of supersensory perception, and where dialogue often occurred between various entities. Anthropologist Roger Wescott writes:

> Moreover, most mythic traditions concur in asserting that, in the Golden Age, human beings associated easily and often with beings that were discarnate or only intermittently incarnate, ranging from awesome cosmic deities to playful local spirits.[4]

Eliade, likewise, noted in his research that ancient myths spoke of a friendship between animals and humans, with them even having knowledge of their respective languages.

Eliade speculates that the shamanic imagery and/or visions of human transformation into an animal may be a metaphorical account of reestablishing a connection that was lost at the dawn of time. According to Eliade, the shaman goes into a transcendental state in order to 'abolish the present human condition,' which is regarded as a resultant state from the Fall, and thus reenter into the natural condition of primordial man as it was during the Golden Age.[5] Heinberg writes:

> Paradise may be seen as serving a specific function, as a *design for living* embedded in the circuitry of human consciousness. All biological organisms, including human beings, contain elements of design. . . . Perhaps we also contain within us a neurological or psychic program for the optimal design of social and spiritual relations between ourselves, the Cosmos, and Nature—a design of telepathic oneness and interspecies communion that represents the goal toward which our individual and collective experience would naturally tend to unfold.[6]

Heinberg is suggesting here that memories of paradise may not only, or necessarily, refer to a physical reality or time, but serve to activate and catalyze human neurological and psychic functioning into continued evolutionary growth. The memory, then, is not only as a remembrance of things past, but may also function as a design wired into us as a social and spiritual guide during dark ages — those times when our psychic, and thus also physical, states are low and separated from a sacred source.

Similarly, various religious, spiritual, and indigenous traditions all refer to this rupture (our 'Fall') as a descent into greed, egoism, fear, and selfishness. It is a state where the focus is almost entirely upon gross materialism. Gnostic, Hindu, and Buddhist traditions also refer to humanity forgetting its true purpose; of how the distraction of, and attraction to, the physical world produces a continued state of separation. Teutonic Norse myths state that a renewal of the world would only come after great destruction in which a period of chaos and disorder would arise that would see humans commit many degrading and tragic acts. There are also numerous accounts in ancient and sacred texts that depict the theme of cyclic destruction and renewal; from biblical accounts, Hindu scriptures, and Tibetan narratives. Our myths, stories, and narratives may serve to remind us of where we have been, and to where we need to return. Yet can we rely solely on the old myths, or are we now in need of new mythologies? After all, where did all the gods go?

NEW MYTHOLOGIES

It has been said that our old gods are dead or dying. The many gods of times past were abandoned in favor of the one god concept with the rise of monotheistic religions. With this shift away from multiple gods — gods who played a more direct, intervening role in human affairs — a new individualized sense of self and self-consciousness began to emerge. The spiritual focus was now not on the interaction with multiple gods, but on a relation with a single source that was transcendent and beyond the lowly human. Humanity no longer played ball together with their godly caretakers, and so the human psyche slowly became separated from a close communion with the gods. This psychic bond or participation between cosmic forces and the human soul gradually became severed, leaving the individual to their own devices and further away from a distant god.

This break from the interventionist gods is likely to have played a role in the shift of human consciousness towards its own self-involvement, which amplified the presence and dominance of the ego. Along with this shift came the art of personal reflection and the manifestation of individual thinking. This can be seen in the external transition from ancient Egyptian spiritual traditions to the human philosophy of the Greeks. This marked a shift toward knowledge as grasped by the human mind, and thus led to the increased belief that no gods were needed to understand such lofty concepts.

Divinity, the realm of the gods, became a place to which certain elite human minds could broker access. This was seen as liberating the human soul from the direct and all-powerful influence of the gods in daily life. A new independence arose that preceded an era of increasing human autonomy at play within a material world. The human being was now born into an environment where the gods had withdrawn. Humanity was now left to stand on its own spiritual feet, and to learn to navigate through a world given over to them by their gods. And yet it was precisely this kind of environment which made it possible for an individual to develop a sense of full responsibility for their own behavior and spiritual state. The soul life of the human had now become their own task to contend with, and could no longer be seen as under the sway of external transcendental forces. Although this shift placed the onus of development upon the human self, it also dissolved the reciprocal understanding between human and cosmos.

By defining ourselves as independent of the gods, we also defined ourselves as similarly being separated from nature. This process of separation between our interior and exterior lives was drawn out over centuries, and further exacerbated through orthodox religious thinking, scientific rationalism, Cartesian philosophy, and attitudes to the human body. We are now coming to the end of the influence of the Greco-Roman, Judeo-Christian era. As philosopher Jeremy Naydler notes:

> It has achieved its purpose, which was to make us more individuated, more self- rather than god-centered in our soul-life, and thus more free. But now there is a need to become aware again of inner, spiritual realities, but to become aware of them grounded in our own sense of self and with a clear and discriminating intelligence with which we can once more turn toward them.[7]

Individual selfhood came at a great cost. In fact, it could only come about when the previous gods had faded from human consciousness. And yet from this came the emergence of self-consciousness, the focus on individual selfhood, and the possibility for self-transcendence through individual inner work. That is, to take the path back toward a cosmic, sacred communion through self-volition and individual choice. This path back to the gods (the sacred source) does not imply going out there to reach them in some realm beyond, but rather suggests allowing them back into the human psyche. This means receiving the sacred connection once again within the inner life or self of the individual. We could phrase it as *bringing the sacred impulse back down into material life* – the resacralization of the material plane. It could be said that human destiny is to know the infinite without leaving the finite. Both exist simultaneously, and both are necessary.

Spirit is not recognized by it being something *other* than the material, but by overcoming its *otherness*. It is implicit within all material forms, and is in communion with all entities. In the sacred traditions, spirit is a living recognition not an inanimate one. That is, sacred spirit wishes to be known beyond its otherness. Our multiple gods, as depth psychology informs us, also represent aspects of the human psyche. Astrology places a similar pattern upon the planets, as their alignment influences psychic correspondences and can affect humans physically, mentally, and emotionally.

In some of the most ancient spiritual traditions that came out of Egypt and Mesopotamia thousands of years ago, the realm of spirit existed in a transcendental pure form beyond matter. It was human destiny for the privileged, capable few to ascend through rigorous trial and initiation toward this *otherworld* and seek a connection with it so that it could manifest through them on the material plane. Hence, such cultures were star-orientated, as this represented a source beyond the terrestrial earth.

In more modern times, the implication has shifted to a view that sees spirit as having its destiny to become implicated in matter. Together, spirit and matter form the necessary communion. The respiritualization, or resacralization, of the material world must come about through humanity's involvement. Humans must embrace the cosmos within themselves and bring it down to earth, so to speak. This is now a mass endeavor, which suggests that the time for the elite, special few initiates is over. In other words, where once a higher state of consciousness was first developed through exceptional individuals, it is now to be developed through the masses by receptive individuals and communities connecting together across physical and temporal boundaries.

A resacralization is required on a global scale — a sacred revival for our times. As I suggest later in this book, this very thing may be brought into play within our global civilization *if* we transition to a genuine relationship with our developing technologies. Likewise, the natural world is not an obstacle that needs to be overcome if we are to strive towards a sacred communion and understanding. On the contrary, the natural world is itself the playground through which sacred energies move, and within which lies the *soul of the world*.

The old mythologies placed the gods within the supernatural world, where nature was something to move through and beyond. Yet the old mythologies are no longer with us, for they no longer serve the same purpose. They too have been transcended, for we are in a different era, an altogether different temporal and spatial state. The old mythological world of archetypal energies has now been fused into an order where the supernatural, the natural, and the human mind and soul merge together. We are participating in bringing the sacred back into the material realm, in bringing the gods back home. The sacred source is to be encountered through ourselves, not within another world — through normal human consciousness rather than its denial. We can say that 'humanity has entered a new stage in the unfolding cosmological drama, and that this stage is to do with the infinite rediscovering itself within the sphere of the finite.'[8]

From these ashes a new mythology must arise, one that has been gestating within the inner reaches of humankind for some time already. It has been suggested that we are in a battle for the Western soul, as we have been largely sleeping through crisis after crisis of the spirit. A new mythology is rapidly becoming both a social and spiritual necessity, as our old frameworks and worldviews dissolve from usefulness. Mythologies have the power to conduct and guide us through our lifetimes, as a companion upon the psychospiritual journey of transformation. A mythology is a set of figures and symbols that can reflect and shape a state of mind; they can serve as a perceptual framework. They can be our filters and our friends, but they neither belong to us nor any particular locale. They are available for everyone, and are beyond the individual mind. According to Joseph Campbell, arguably one of the most respected mythologists of the twentieth century:

> The life of a mythology derives from the vitality of its symbols as metaphors delivering, not simply the idea, but a sense of actual participation in such a realization of transcendence, infinity, and abundance . . . The first and most essential service of a mythology is this one, of opening the mind and heart to the utter wonder of all being. And the second service, then, is cosmologi-

cal: of representing the universe and whole spectacle of nature, both as known to the mind and as beheld by the eye.[9]

Mythology then should serve to assist participation in our own transcendence amid the spectacle of the cosmos. Unfortunately, it is when mythologies become locked in as social, political, and religious control systems that the human developmental path becomes distorted and muddy underfoot.

Myths emphasize commonality and offer us a transcendental communion, as long as we don't corrupt them into further mental prisons. It is essential therefore that the new mythologies for a sacred revival inspire within humanity a wish for interiorizing the cosmological impulse that is pervasive and which irradiates our reality.

In the next chapter I shall be bringing us back home, from the past into the present, as we continue the unfolding journey along the revival. Now we must seek some answers within this thing called modernity.

Notes

[1] Carl Gustav Jung, *Memories, Dreams, Reflections* (London: Flamingo, 1995).

[2] Idries Shah, *Thinkers of the East* (London: Jonathan Cape, 1971), 123.

[3] Richard Heinberg, *Memories & Visions of Paradise: Exploring the Universal Myth of a Lost Golden Age* (Northamptonshire: The Aquarian Press, 1990), xxviii.

[4] Quoted in Heinberg, *Memories & Visions of Paradise*, 210.

[5] Mircea Eliade, *The Sacred and the Profane* (New York: Harper & Row, 1961).

[6] Heinberg, *Memories & Visions of Paradise*, 240-1.

[7] Jeremy Naydler, *The Future of the Ancient World: Essays on the History of Consciousness* (Rochester, VT: Inner Traditions, 2009), 147.

[8] Naydler, *The Future of the Ancient World*, 258.

[9] Joseph Campbell, *The Inner Reaches of Outer Space: Metaphor as Myth and as Religion* (Novato, CA: New World Library, 2012), xx.

4

JUGGLING WITH SACRED TOTEMS: MODERNITY AND BEYOND

The Age of Reason is visibly drawing to an end.
— Sri Aurobindo, *The Human Cycle*

The twenty-first century will be spiritual or it will not be.
— André Malraux

This thing called modernity is indeed a capricious puzzle full of contradictions and contortions. Perhaps we are, as Sri Aurobindo tells us, now coming to the end of our reason. And yet we needed a good bout of reason to have arrived where we are. The scientific materialism that developed from our Scientific Revolution has pushed the world toward greater physical unification. We are now more connected through our global technologies than ever before. This has helped to create a stronger mental unification across the planet. This greater sense of global communion will assist in bridging the past, into the present, and toward an unprecedented future.

Our current cultural transformation, which some have referred to as the Modernity Project, is greater than the transformation we went through during the industrial revolutions, since it involves shifting into a global culture rather than a national one. We could compare it to how the Renaissance shifted from medievalism to modernism, or even before that (if we wish to take the bigger picture) to the beginnings of agrarianism. And yet there is something unique and exceptional about what the world and human civilization is going through right now, and that is the question of time. While the agrarian revolution took thousands of years, and the Renaissance and the industrial revolutions took place over more than a century, our current cultural transformation is occurring within the space of a single individual's lifetime. This is an unprecedented rate of change. This also suggests that our individual lives, and our expression of consciousness, are now very much a part of the planetary transformation underway.

Individual human consciousness is part of our complex cultural ecologies to a higher degree than our animistic ancestors. And after the industrial revolutions, with our machinist technologies, we are also seeing how technology is increasingly becoming an appendage to human consciousness. Also, amplified by emerging digital technologies, human consciousness can have a more dynamic impact upon earthly affairs greater than has ever been possible before in history. And yet, despite all this, we have entered the third millennium in a state of befuddlement and confusion.

We have been losing our understanding of who we are as a species, and our sense of purpose and direction. We ambled, disastrously and dangerously, out of the twentieth century into a new millennial era. Globalization, as an infant stage upon the way to a planetary civilization, has made many immature and lame steps. Historian Eric Hobsbawm saw the end of the twentieth century as 'that of a world which lost its bearings and slid into instability and crisis.'[1] And yet modernity is just a name for a place where we think we are, possessing something we are not sure we have. In this sense, perhaps it is the best playing field to be on for the visible/tangible and invisible/intangible worlds to mix and merge. It's the meeting point of the void with the inferno.

By focusing on the twentieth century, I am basing my review upon what is commonly referred to as late modernity, principally 1870–1970, the main period of industrialization from the Second Industrial Revolution to the recent phase of globalization. From the 1970s onwards, the Western, developed world was dealing with the post-1968 social revolutions and the onslaught of postmodernism in the arts and sciences.

Another commentator on the twentieth century, Italian philosopher Julius Evola, described how that century had given us 'the sense of a *tabula rasa*, the cosmic silence, the void, the end of a whole epoch.'[2] For Evola, the whole historical process of modernity could be likened to Nietzsche's famous dictum on the death of God, whereby unbelief became a daily reality, leading to 'a desacralization of existence and a total rift with the world.'[3] With human life having lost its reference to transcendence and the notion of the sacred, according to Evola, we then descend purely to human morality:

> For some time, a good part of Western humanity has considered it a natural thing for existence to lack any real meaning, and for it not to be ordered by any higher principle, arranging their lives in the most bearable and least disagreeable way they can. Of course this has its counterpart and inevitable consequence in an inner life that is more and more reduced, formless, feeble, and elusive.[4]

Evola, like many others, believed that an inertia had crept into modern society, and that the modern pursuit of progress had not had a corresponding development in the inner realm. The result was that human beings inevitably found themselves with a hollow space inside. This space became the perfect seedbed for the dazzling distractions and enticing attractions that were the hallmark of modernity's consumptive excesses. Within such an environment we wonder whether we may find ourselves waking up to a world where the dream is still dreaming itself and we can no longer distinguish what is real.

However, modernity may have been a necessary phase in which we could experience the loss of mythic connection to the cosmos; and with it, a loss of connection to our universal soul and sense of cosmic significance and personal meaning. Through modernity and its sibling postmodernity, we are experiencing a rearrangement of meaning and a reevaluation of the role of the individual. Theologian Paul Tillich observed that the greatest sin of modernism was not evil but rather 'the barren triviality that preoccupies us.'[5] Through modernity's influence we have been all too easily appeased by seeking inadequate answers to life's meaning, as if we were taught to be satiated by a half-full stomach of sugar and spice. The remaining hungry space is then often filled with trivial distractions and numbing affirmations.

Modernity did not seek to align itself with a greater wisdom beyond its own realm, it sought acquisition rather than alignment. It sought to dictate, and thus control, its own rhythms as well as the rhythms of nature. Modernity did not seek for the essential, and so could not hope to be anything other than temporary. French philosopher René Guénon took the view that in order to 'grasp the true significance of the modern world . . . it is necessary to be entirely detached from the mentality which is its special characteristic and to avoid being affected by it in the smallest degree.'[6] The danger, it appeared, was in being infected by the dreaded sickness of modernity and begetting a modern mind that 'shows an alarming degree of dissociation and psychological confusion.'[7] At least through myth we could relate to and release our inner currents, yet in modernity we have let these unchecked inner currents manifest in dangerously tangible ways.

Modernity has been the playing field for humankind's unconscious desires and urges—a kaleidoscopic experimentation of our inner states and their projected manifestations. Throughout the twentieth century, the inner world of human beings began to be opened, explored, analyzed, and experimented with alongside Western industrial and technological development. By the end of the twentieth century, both had reached a peak in their self-destructiveness. We had shifted around with our sacred totems and made a modern art smorgasbord out of them—displayed pretentiously in museums and sold to rich bidders with more cash than sense. If it's true that modernity and its recent antecedents have muffled the call of transcendental mystery, then it is equally true that they have thus made transformation both a more needed and yet more difficult promise. The call for a re-communion with the sacred source is now one that must inevitably begin within the self. In what may seem like a paradox, another current running through modernity was the growth in the psychological evolution of the human self.

Psychoanalysis, developed in Vienna in the 1890s by Sigmund Freud, began percolating into mainstream circles during the early part of the twentieth century. The theories of Freud, Jung, Reich, and other psychoanalysts were changing how people regarded human behavior and the parameters of human thinking. Early childhood impacts, experiences, repressions, and sexuality were all now being unearthed as contributing to contours that carved out a sense of the human self. What happened in these external experiences was recognized as being a manifestation of what was going on inside a person's inner realm.

It was thus a period when the collective unconscious was becoming a conscious part of the collective mind. This coincided with a zeitgeist in the second half of the twentieth century as the East came to meet the West through the newfound popularity of Eastern teachings (Buddhism, Taoism, Sufism, etc.) and the experimental playfulness of mind-altering processes. During this period of cultural experimentation, a new form of psychological consciousness was being explored. Through psychoanalysis and depth psychology, the 1950s and 1960s opened up new areas of self-evaluation. People were increasingly exploring their own feelings through self-reflection and the interior gaze. There was also a surge of interest in the esoteric arts of alchemy, Hermeticism, Kabbalah, and Gnosticism.

These changes all correlated with a greater shift towards individual responsibility, a deepened sense of self, and psychological reflection. As psychologist James Hollis notes:

> The single biggest shift in human culture, that which denotes the nature of modernism, is that the world has become psychological; that is, the logos of meaning of soul is everywhere manifest. This means that we have lost both simple beliefs and external authorities and are driven to recognize that the same energies driving the cosmos also course within.[8]

This indeed is welcome news. All is not lost. It suggests that we have entered a psychological transitional period where the eventual aim is of the transformation of humanity. This naturally brings many certainties into question, and many unknowns into play, which is exactly where postmodernism comes in.

POSTMODERNISM: WHAT HAPPENED TO THE SELF?

We are living in a new world, a world that does not know how to define itself by what it is, but only by what it has just now ceased to be.
—Walter Truett Anderson

Postmodernism, as the name suggests, arrived blazing in at the end of the period of late modernity somewhere around the later end of the mid-twentieth century. Also, as the name suggests, it is an era that so far has been incapable of its own definition. Rather than a clearly defined age with its own specific recognition, it identifies itself by being 'post-something,' which suggests it is following on from the past but may not yet be fully in the present. It's as if it's in the waiting room between what it once was and what it still can be and has the potential to become.

So far it seems that the postmodern culture is an era for the heightening of the individual—a society where everything is personalized and the importance is on the varieties of the self. Postmodern society has no more idols or taboos, no sustained image of itself, no great historical framing. It is a void filled with experimental uncertainties. This uncertainty is what defines postmodernism, both as a culture and as a body of art and representation. It suggests a lack of metanarrative, where threads and narratives exist as simulacra of what is real. Postmodernism stands as a questioning of history, a fragmentation of truths, a commodity fetishism and a spiritual consumerism—a sociocultural movement that turned itself into a worldview.*

This worldview is a triumph over reason. It fragments and destabilizes reason and also fragments greater truths into lesser uncertain truths. These filaments of uncertainty are the framework upon which social systems and cultural identities have been built. Postmodernism is a reaction against an ordered world of irrational faith (medieval, industrial) giving us a conception of the world that, since the twentieth century, has been up for grabs. In some ways we are living in a merry-

---
*   See my essays "Spirituality vs. Consumerism," http://kingsleydennis.com/spirituality-vs-consumerism/; and "Spirituality vs. Fetishism," http://kingsleydennis.com/spirituality-vs-fetishism/

go-round entertainment malaise (which avant-garde artists may interpret as a merry-up-down mayonnaise!). In this hodgepodge of disordered vision, there appears no great reason for our existence, which goes unnoticed even by the vast universe. Some may interpret this as the universe saying that there's no grand reason for life, so just get on with things and have fun. If this is indeed who we are, then the picture it gives us is nothing special. Or, as philosopher Gary Lachman says:

> Postmodern thought has set us free. We have been liberated from the demand to be great and relieved of the obligation to be something better than ourselves. We can embrace our mediocrity with a good conscience and sleep better at night. . . . Postmodernism 'ironizes' out all questions of meaning. It reduces everything to the 'been there, done that' mentality, and shrinks the world to a theory of everything that can fit on a T-shirt. It lets us off the hook. We no longer have to be good, just good enough.[9]

The consequence of postmodernism is that there is no sense of a true self; the individual is a decentered cluster of temporary uncertainties. There are no grand narratives, and all world systems and views are merely relative and unstable. This smorgasbord of possibilities is oiled by an underlying lubricant of nihilism.

Of course, meaning and truth are never absolute in the human realm, as they are sociocultural constructions. However, the deconstructive nature of the postmodern era may have, somewhat paradoxically, confined us more to the trappings of language and context rather than freeing us. We must be careful we do not find ourselves bound and wound up in greater verbosity and verbs of doing rather than states of being. The knowledge that imbibes our cultural institutions pushes at the boundaries of the exoteric while neglecting the esoteric world of the human self. Postmodernism, our indefinable quagmire hanging on desperately at the end of late modernity, has managed to further desacralize the human experience. It reminds us of the tale of the little boy who dissected a fly by pulling off its wings, then its legs, before finally crying out, 'But where is the fly?'

Whether wingless, legless, or rootless, all these states foster meaninglessness; and the lack of meaning in life is a soul-sickness that is not life-inducing. For all the calls and cries of liberty and selfhood that postmodernism places on placards and in shop windows, we have failed to grasp that the genuine source of liberty lies *within*. The 'self' has been taken for granted, along with infusion teas, macrobiotic food, and T-shirt slogans.

The greatest danger now comes from ourselves as we stand on the threshold of the sacred revival. Our psyche is in danger of atrophying if we do not soon reconnect it with a world soul and a thriving cosmos. Our most virulent epidemics are not from physical disease but from a psychical 'dis-ease' and dismemberment. Postmodernism loves to deconstruct and take things apart, yet when it arrives at a huge space where there's nothing more, it lacks the know-how and the punch to put things back together again. Postmodernism is savvy and flashy like a slick dessert full of empty calories. Ultimately it dissolves in the mouth leaving no lasting flavor. As the psychotherapist Carl Jung observed:

> Modern man believes that he can do as he pleases and is perturbed that inexplicable anxieties plague him. True to his rationalistic bias, he has tried all the usual remedies—diets, exercise programs, studying inspirational literature—and only reluctantly admits that he can't seem to find a way to live a meaningful life.[10]

Our separation from an enchanted world, a participatory cosmos, has come at a grave cost. It would take many volumes to list the woes of our world—its inequalities, barbarism, political insanity, cultural psychosis, environmental devastation, and spiritual amnesia. We have blinded ourselves to the sacred treasures within and without, and have replaced them with modern demons like restlessness, ennui, apathy, disorientation, dietary stupidity, and nagging neuroses. Humanity once placed its demons within the rocks, woods, mountains, and rivers. Now the very same demons have placed themselves inside the psyche of humanity.

There is no real excuse we can give ourselves for spiritual stagnation, since it has to begin with us. We are the alpha and omega of our own journey. No government on earth is going to provide genuine spiritual welfare, nor should they. Postmodernism titillated and distracted us from without, yet we've been doing pretty much the same from within for much longer. The rediscovery of our sacred communion between the human being, the soul of the world, and a magical, intelligent cosmos is an imperative which must be accomplished if we wish to preserve, prolong, and progress human civilization. Again citing the wisdom of Carl Jung:

> When a man is fifty years old, only one part of his being has existed for half a century. The other part, which also lives in his psyche, may be millions of years old. . . . Contemporary man is but the latest ripe fruit on the tree of the human race. None of us knows what we know.[11]

To reiterate the André Malraux quote at the beginning of the chapter, *'The twenty-first century will be spiritual or it will not be.'* There can be no dull future, it is not permissible. There needs to be more knowing of what we know, and less forgetting and dismissing. We will reconnect with the sacred or we will stagnate. The magical, mysterious sacred revival is already underway, it just isn't paraded by the mainstream yet. But the spores are seeding all over the holy ground of this blessed planet. It will come to pass—it has already been born.

Within the topsy-turvy tumbling and spinning of the postmodern melee, amid the deconstructions and abandoned metanarratives, lies an immense, erratic, erotic, and abstract playfulness. The diversity of the postmodern experimentalism allows anything to come into incarnation. As writer and cultural experimenter William S. Burroughs famously remarked, '*Nothing is true, everything is permitted.*' As we shall explore in chapter six, a thread of discord remains central to the modern narrative as a way of allowing new permutations to arise, breathe, and morph. And yet, as Leonard Shlain so aptly pointed out, when trapped in the center of a spinning washing machine, it is difficult for anyone so positioned to appreciate that the clothes tumbling violently about are becoming cleaner. Yet within this tumbling manner of cleansing there is an inner voice wishing to be heard.

THE PSYCHE CALLS OUT

Let's be honest, the call to be heard—for meaning, significance, or rightful value—cries out from the depths of the human self. The longing for purpose lashes out at the faceless facade of an anaesthetized modern life. Somewhere within our cultural creative mix we feel an impulse that pulls us ever nearer to a social milieu where the inner landscape is acknowledged and expressed. We wish for a future where a new vitality arouses the sensuous, the psychic, and the communal; where self-actualization becomes the actual, and individuation replaces individualism. We long, whether outwardly or secretly, for the great wealth of diversity that will overtake the humdrum homogeneity of franchised global commercialism, where artisan enterprises will regain their value over the flotsam of factory fabrications. We long for this future culture that, as Morris Berman notes, 'will have a greater tolerance for the strange, the nonhuman, for diversity of all sorts, both within the personality and without.'[12]

The playground of postmodernity appears to offer a canvas for us to experiment upon until we find a new legitimating expression for human life. It offers a canvas where a sacred and empathic consciousness can surface, and upon which we can nurture a relationship to something deeper and more permanent than ourselves. And this relationship, being of a sacred kind, will reinstate the human and cosmic order which has, for all time, existed in entanglement. As Rene Guenon put it:

> The human order and the cosmic order are not in reality separated, as they are nowadays all too readily imagined to be; they are on the contrary closely bound together, in such a way that each continuously reacts on the other and so that there is always correspondence between their respective states.[13]

Within the fragmentation of the postmodern condition we are being asked to put ourselves back together again. As if mirroring our Fall (the descent and ascent process) we are thrown the hand of reconstituting ourselves, and thus given the opportunity to recombine or retrace the jigsaw pieces of our soul. This sacred sense of the self, if I may call it that, involves the sense of having lived our own life as well and as fully as possible, and includes the deep gnosis that we have some linkage with a larger order of meaning. As sentient and soulful human beings, we thrive for some connection with the mystery that courses through history, and which has from time immemorial animated the individual and collective spirit. As psychologist James Hollis says, 'To reach the end of one's life and to know that one has not truly taken the journey is more terrible than any terrors one would have had to face on the way.'[14]

And now our sacred journey continues further into the rabbit hole of revival without, it is hoped, the terrible terrors that accompany the realization of a flaccid life. Instead, it is the knowing, accepting, and the seeking out the sacred aspects of life that bring the revitalizing energies surging and coursing through our spirit veins. But hold on, we still haven't yet fully navigated ourselves out of the wormhole of postmodernism. The whirling merry-go-round of popular culture wheezes on . . .

Notes

[1] Eric Hobsbawm, *The Age of Extremes: The Short Twentieth Century 1914-1991* (London: Abacus, 1995), 403.

[2] Julius Evola, *Ride the Tiger: A Survival Manual for the Aristocrats of the Soul* (Rochester, VT: Inner Traditions, 2003/1961), 24.

[3] Evola, *Ride the Tiger*, 16.

[4] Evola, *Ride the Tiger*, 21.

[5] Quoted in James Hollis, *Tracking the Gods: The Place of Myth in Modern Life* (Toronto, Canada: Inner City Books, 1995), 61.

[6] Rene Guenon, *The Reign of Quantity and the Signs of the Times* (New Delhi: Munshiram Manoharlal Publishers, 2000/1953), 8.

[7] Meredith Sabini, Ed., *C. G. Jung on Nature, Technology & Modern Life* (Berkeley, CA: North Atlantic Books, 2008), 127.

[8] Hollis, *Tracking the Gods*, 148.

[9] Gary Lachman, *The Caretakers of the Cosmos: Living Responsibly in an Unfinished World* (Edinburgh: Floris Books, 2013), 209-10.

[10] Sabini, *C. G. Jung on Nature, Technology & Modern Life*, 16.

[11] Sabini, *C. G. Jung on Nature, Technology & Modern Life*, 196.

[12] Morris Berman, *The Reenchantment of the World* (Ithaca, New York: Cornell University Press, 1981), 275.

[13] Guenon, *The Reign of Quantity and the Signs of the Times*, 140.

[14] Hollis, *Tracking the Gods*, 149.

5

HERE BE DRAGONS:
FROM POSTHISTORIC TO POSTHUMAN

The collective psyche seems to be in the grip of a powerful archetypal dynamic in which the long-alienated modern mind is breaking through, out of the contractions of its birth process, out of what Blake called its 'mind-forg'd manacles,' to rediscover its intimate relationship with nature and the larger cosmos.
— Richard Tarnas, *Cosmos and Psyche*

Reality, it seems, has been deregulated, and nothing is business as usual anymore. . . . As ancient mapmakers used to mark on the watery unknown, 'Here be dragons.'
— Erik Davis, *Techgnosis*

Here be dragons, indeed. Our exploration into reality has passed the post of no return and is venturing into uncharted waters where dragons are being unleashed from the human imagination like never before. The results may be enthralling, but not always on the right track. As discussed in chapter two, there are indications that human civilization and consciousness is on an upward developing momentum (the rising arc of the Dwapara Yuga). As part of this transition there is a corresponding heightening of mental faculties alongside clarity of understanding, which includes knowledge of the finer forces at work within the cosmos. I speculate that this upswing corresponds to a resurgence in the sacred revival, which is reanimating our relationship to the world around us. And this includes how we experiment in our interactions with not only the environment but also our bodies. In this chapter I will explore these themes, looking at memes of metaprogramming to post-body scenarios — all in the framework of a human search along the sacred path of understanding our very *selves*.

American writer Philip K. Dick is famous mostly for his science fiction books that question the nature and validity of our reality matrix. In 'The Android and the Human,' a speech that Dick gave in the early 1970s, he spoke about this blurring of the boundaries between body and environment:

> Our environment, and I mean our man-made world of machines, artificial constructs, computers, electronic systems, interlinking homeostatic components — all of this is in fact beginning more and more to possess what the earnest psychologists fear the primitive sees in his environment: animation. In a very real sense our environment is becoming alive, or at least quasi-alive, and in ways specifically and fundamentally analogous to ourselves.[1]

The relation of the human body with its environment is increasingly being reconfigured as a site for a new magical animism, as distinct from the previous archaic notion of animism. Writer-philosopher Erik Davis has referred to this as a sort of 'techno-animism' whereby we give life to our technologies based on our imaginations.² This new configuration is no longer about technologies and us, but rather our technological bodies that now inhabit our 'techno-imaginal' realm. The body is coming back into vogue as a site for experience and experimentation, as a vessel that interacts, intercedes, and interprets the sacred, mystical reality matrix that encloses us. As modern quantum science has now aptly demonstrated, we do not inhabit a subject-object type of *us-and-it* world.* All materiality is enmeshed within a quantum entangled universe, and our bodies are somatically communicating with this energy field simultaneously.

Much of the Western spiritual (Gnostic) mystical practice is interpreted as a somatically-felt experience. The body is the instrument that receives and grounds the experience, whether it be in terms of the 'great flash,' 'illuminating light,' or the 'bodily rush.' The body is the human instrument for attracting and centralizing (receiving, transcribing, and sometimes transferring) developmental energy. There are many 'bodies' in spiritual-mystic traditions, including the etheric, the spiritual, the ecstatic, the subtle, the higher, and others, so that the purely physical, material body is recognized as the densest and least mobile of them all.

---

*   See *Dawn of the Akashic Age: New Consciousness, Quantum Resonance, and the Future of the World* by Ervin Laszlo and Kingsley L. Dennis.

As cultural historian Morris Berman has noted, the body in history has always been a site of focus.[3] It has helped define the experience of the self/other and the outer/inner, and is a material vessel for the spiritual impulse. Our earlier ancestors, who exhibited more of an animist relationship to the world, saw less distinction between the physical body and its environment. The rise of the philosophy of dualism, which was supported by the mechanistic worldview, saw our modern societies further strengthen the mind-body rift. This was publicly endorsed by organized religions that have been quick to spurn and even demonize the body.

Many so-called modern societies around the world have, at one time or another, attempted to suppress the power and expression of the human body. The body has always been a site for the convergence of power and control. Perhaps no one in recent times has done more to expose this body-power relationship than the work of French philosopher Michel Foucault.* Foucault has deconstructed, in the body of work that he refers to as a critical history of modernity, how the body has been fought over as a site of power. The physical body is a location of resistance against the establishment. It is a fixed place where an individual can be located, found, and held accountable. If we cannot escape from our bodies then, it seems we are forever within the system. The human body, as part of the social system, has

---

*　　See especially Michel Foucault's *Discipline and Punish.*

always been taken to represent the *form* of something, as a socially tangible entity. We have bodies in terms of social institutions, such as the body politic, or the social body, the scientific body, the medical body, or the body of an organization, etc. The once sacred site of the body, which was the vessel for somatic spiritual experiences, has become the subject of control and suppression.

In Gnostic terms the body's site of power has been referred to as those of the 'sleepers' and 'wakers.' Sleepers are those whose conscious self has yet to break through the layers of the body's social conditioning. The somatic spiritual experience has been seen as a threat to hierarchical societies because it exists beyond their bounds of power. This is one reason why ecstatic experiences, whether through spiritual or other means, have been suppressed, outlawed, and discredited by religions and mainstream institutions alike. Ecstatic experiences that can break down thinking patterns and conditioning structures are unnerving for institutions of sociopolitical power. How can you control, regulate, and discipline a body, energy, or experience that has no physical location? Such intangible forces, such as the power of baraka, is positively infectious and beyond bounds.* As Berman notes:

---

* Baraka, a prominent concept in Islamic mysticism, refers to a flow of grace and spiritual power that can be transmitted.

> The goal of the Church (any church) is to obtain a monopoly on this vibratory experience, to channel it into its own symbol system, when the truth is that the somatic response is not the exclusive property of any given religious leader or particular set of symbols.[4]

The spiritual, occult renaissance of the twentieth century strove to rejuvenate and strengthen the presence of the somatic experience. This intangible flow of spiritual blessing, grace, and power is also a resurging undercurrent in the sacred revival.

In more recent times there has been an increasing focus on what is termed the innate consciousness of the body, and which has been revealed through such techniques as muscle testing. It is innate because it is inborn (born in and *of* the body), and it is instinctual. Somatic consciousness then is another word for our intuitive intelligence. As I discussed in a previous book,* many of those now being born into the world are displaying a stronger sense of intuitive intelligence. However, in our modern haste we have, in the words of French philosopher Bruno Latour, never really been modern at all, since we continue to exist in an anthropological matrix where nature and culture cannot be neatly divided. As Latour points out, this matrix is composed of hybrids where natural/cultural, real/imagined, and subject/

---

* See *The Phoenix Generation: A New Era of Connection, Compassion, and Consciousness.*

object merge. Moreover, this hybridity is being further enforced and coalesced through genetic engineering, implants, virtual reality, and NBIC sciences (Nanotechnology, Biotechnology, Information technology, and Cognitive science). Latour is right in saying that humanity has never exited from what he refers to as our premodern ancestors' world. We are, and always have been, a hybrid of body, mind, and environment. Yet unlike Latour, I contest that we are modern — or rather we are past the post of postmodern in how we are merging our lives into a new hybrid fusion.

Our ancestors made no such division between nature and society because their state of consciousness did not allow them to. They simply did not *perceive* it. However, the state of human consciousness today is far different in its capability and lucidity to perceive and acknowledge the relationship with our external world. Yet in our development to be 'modern' we left behind the sacred component of perceiving just how entangled our reality truly is. Yet the succeeding 'postmodern' stage then worked on breaking down these 'perceptions of containment.' As William Irwin Thompson says:

> The project of Modernism was to expel preindustrial magic and mysticism and stabilize consciousness in materialism, but the projects of postmodernism have broken down the walls that once contained us in a solidly materialistic and confidently middle class worldview.[5]

This breakdown has now moved into a more advanced stage with the advent of the Internet and digital technologies. We have now entered what Thompson refers to as the 'astral plane, a bardo realm, in which everything is out there at once, a technologized form of the collective unconscious ... a place where the physical body is either dead or absent.'[6]

Thompson prefers to view this technologized bardo realm, where the physical body is either dead or absent, not as postmodern but as postcivilization or even posthistoric.[7] We are in a new phase of planetary culture where we are no longer simply reacting to emerging technologies, but rather our evolving state of consciousness is drawing forth these new technologies. In other words, it is as if new technologies come into being in accordance with shifting states of human consciousness. Like a good magician, we are pulling new technological innovations out of the hat of our collective consciousness, bringing archetypes into manifestation. Whereas modernity was about coming to our senses in a rather conservative way, the posts we have passed now — whether they be modern, civilization, or historic — are about shifting *beyond our senses*. As one well-placed commentator put it:

> The human being's organism is producing a new complex of organs in response to such a need. In this age of the transcending of time and space, the complex of organs is concerned with the transcending of time and

space. What ordinary people regard as sporadic and occasional bursts of telepathic or prophetic power are . . . nothing less than the first stirrings of these same organs.[8]

As a new historical phase unfolds within the human species as part of a shift toward a planetary civilization, it appears that new needs are giving birth to novel faculties within the human being.

This brings to mind the Richard Tarnas quote that headed up this chapter, where he stated that the once alienated (read 'sacred') mind is now breaking through, as if in a birth process, out of what Blake called its 'mind-forg'd manacles,' to 'rediscover its intimate relationship with nature and the larger cosmos.' Note that Tarnas said 'rediscover,' suggesting it is a recovery, a revival, and not a new birth. The sacred revival of which I speak is literally carving out a new topography for itself.

HYBRID LANDSCAPES

Our millennial era is still trying to decide how to define and view the physical, biological body. At this stage the landscape is literally littered with a thousand voices, all howling *'for the ancient heavenly connection to the starry dynamo in the machinery of night,'* as Allen Ginsberg wrote in his poem *Howl*. Some voices see the human body as a hindrance upon the evolutionary journey toward an immortal society that is destined for the stars. Others view it as a field for experimentation, where it can be tinkered with and adapted toward a genetically modified hybrid. There are still others who see the body as a site to blur the boundaries between the digital and physical worlds. And then there are those voices who view the biological body as undergoing its own intrinsic, built-in modification or upgrade through a self-adapting nervous system, programmed by emerging DNA programs hitherto latent.

In the latter part of the twentieth century we had a wave of trends that all converged upon the mix of the body, spirit, and mind. These streams included the physical (bodily) research fields of cybernetics, computer programming, and artificial intelligence. These streams then interwove with themes of the mind and spirit in psychedelic experimentation (LSD, peyote, etc.), mystical philosophies (Gurdjieff, Castaneda, etc.), and transcendental movements. You would literally need a whole book dedicated to this topic alone to even begin to make a credible dent into this yellow brick road bricolage of body-mind-spirit convergences.

Just to give a slight taste from the tip of the iceberg, I will ever so briefly mention how the emergence of computing and computer terminology gave rise to notions of programming—and metaprogramming—the human body as a biocomputer. This image was reinforced by Dr. John C. Lilly's book *Programming and Metaprogramming in the Human Biocomputer*, which described some of his experiments on human consciousness and human-dolphin communication. Metaprogramming became a core theme of the writings of Timothy Leary and Robert Anton Wilson, who produced such works as *Exo-Psychology: A Manual on the Use of the Human Nervous System According to the Instructions of the Manufacturers* and *Prometheus Rising* respectively. Both these works discuss an eight-circuit model of consciousness that is part of a path in neurological evolution. Both authors, Leary especially, took it upon themselves to evolve a philosophy stating that the future evolution of human civilization was encoded in our DNA. Hence, the new sacred technology is our nervous system itself, and our DNA is already hardwired for evolutionary mutation.

Similarly, running through some of these streams were the ideas of Caucasian mystic G. I. Gurdjieff, who spoke of the human being in terms of a 'man-machine' that was asleep to life and could be triggered into wakeful activation. Leary, as if in Gurdjieffian overtones, would call for humanity to 'wake up, mutate, and ascend.'[9] The new sacred magic had mutated into practices (rituals) to reprogram the apparatus that receives, according to the authors, our biofields as well as human consciousness—namely, DNA. Interestingly, recent advances in quantum biology have outlined how DNA emits biophotons that produce a coherent biological field that may be susceptible to impact and influence (read 'reprogramming' here).*

Whether or not the new game in town was actively to epigenetically reprogram the DNA through a fusion of transcendental and/or psychedelic practices, it was very much about work on oneself. Gurdjieff's program of study, called The Fourth Way, was a blend of Eastern dervish yoga with Western scientism. As Gurdjieff famously proclaimed, 'Take the understanding of the East and the knowledge of the West and then seek.' This blend of Eastern understanding and Western knowledge became known among its adherents simply as The Work.

The Western melting pot of sacred angst and survivalist spirituality saw an emerg**ence of similar motifs such as E. J. Gold's *The Human Biological Machine as a Transformational Apparatus*. The Western playing field in the second half of the twentieth century was open to a new politics of experimentation and confrontation and it involved the inner spaces of the body and the mind. Robert S. de Ropp aptly called it the Master Game in his book *Master Game: Pathways to Higher Consciousness Beyond the Drug Experience*. For a sense of what was

---

* See also my paper "Quantum Consciousness: Reconciling Science and Spirituality Toward Our Evolutionary Future(s)," *World Futures*, 2010, 511–524.
** See Esalen: America and the Religion of No Religion by Jeffrey J. Kripal.

bubbling up around this Master Game sacred revival, in the United States especially, one needs to understand a history of the Esalen Institute, cofounded by Michael Murphy and Richard Price on the California shores. An excellent if exhaustive study of the body-mind matrix based upon the fizzy, fired-up tropes of the time is Michael Murphy's *The Future of the Body: Explorations into the Further Evolution of Human Nature*. These explorations, however, were all based on expanding and amplifying the potentials of our current human, biological bodies and minds. That was before the computer trope really got going and science fiction became research grant.

The rise of the robots literally happened after the Dartmouth Summer Research Project on Artificial Intelligence, in the summer of 1956, announced the beginning of the AI field. College campuses and defense departments suddenly began the earnest journey along the stony research road that finally spawned the controversial concept of consciousness upload. One of the more vocal supporters of this 'mind-in-machine' notion is robotics researcher Hans Moravec. Moravec, whose books include *Mind Children* and *Robot*, outlines a future where the human mind can be uploaded as a precursor to full artificial intelligence. Similarly, cognitive scientist Marvin Minksy (who was one of the 1956 gang who coined the AI field) espoused a philosophy that saw no fundamental difference between humans and machines, which he put forward in such works as *Society of Mind*. Artificial intelligence is uncannily consistent with the Christian belief in resurrection and immortality. Does this make AI research into a sacred enterprise? It does make us wonder. Historian of technology David F. Noble notes also that the AI project is imbued with its own trajectory of transcendence:

> The thinking machine was not, then, an embodiment of what was specifically human, but of what was specifically divine about humans — the immortal mind ... The immortal mind could evolve independently into ever higher forms of artificial life, reunited at last with its origin, the mind of God.[*]

Other streams have been quick to spring up around this fertile theme, including several futurist movements and their manifestos. These have included, but are not limited to, the Upwingers (F. M. Esfandiary), extropians, and transhumanists. Then later on came the high-profile members that announced the Technological Singularity.

In the 1970 F. M. Esfandiary's *Up-Wingers Manifesto* (by now Esfandiary was known as FM-2030) announced our glorious moment in human evolution. According to their manifesto:

---

[*] For more information on this and related issues, visit http://humanityplus.org/

> We *UpWingers* are resigned to nothing. We consider no human problems irreversible—no goals unattainable. For the first time in history we have the ability, the resources, the genius to resolve ALL our age-old problems. Attain ALL our boldest visions.

Similarly, in the 1980s Max More and Natasha Vita-More expounded on extropian principles which later came to be formulated as: perpetual progress, self-transformation, practical optimism, intelligent technology, self-direction, and rational thinking. And for the Mores, intelligent technology meant, 'Applying science and technology creatively and courageously to transcend 'natural' but harmful, confining qualities derived from our biological heritage, culture, and environment.'*

The transhumanist movement is still going strong and is not definable to any one particular group, although Humanity Plus (H+) is one of its most recognized institutions. There are streams and subgroups under the transhumanist umbrella, and yet they all share a similar goal in viewing the human condition as being open to transformation through the use of sophisticated technologies. In other words, the goal is to give humanity a technological upgrade to its current bodily and mental capacities.

From Gurdjieff's 'man-machine,' to Moravec and Minsky, to Max and Natasha Vita-More and Ray

---
*   For more information on this, visit the Extropy Institute at http://extropy.org/

Kurzweil, the list goes on. And recently we have had the call for a new speciation along the Homo sapiens evolutionary line into *Homo evolutis*. In their TED talk and subsequent book, *Homo Evolutis,* Juan Enriquez and Steve Gullans present how we have already gone through twenty-five speciation events before arriving at our current species. Enriquez and Gullans consider it an anomaly to think that no other humanoid will ever evolve; and so they ask the question: 'What would the next human species look like?' They explain, 'We are transitioning from a hominid that is conscious of its environment into one that drastically shapes its own evolution. . . . We are entering a period of hypernatural evolution . . . *Homo evolutis*.'[12]

This brings us back again to Latour's concept of the anthropological matrix where nature and culture is mixed together without clear boundaries. With the NBIC sciences we are meshing our genetic and cultural DNA. We are 3-D printing buildings as well as human body parts. We are now as a species consciously and deliberately experimenting, shaping, and morphing our environments, as well as journeying and mapping our inner spaces. We are the inhabitants and psychonauts of hybrid landscapes. And yet why should all this be part of an observation on the sacred revival? Because this transmutation of the human condition is what we, as a sentient sapien species, have always been doing.

Our early ancestors have been obsessed with the transmutation of the human body and mind since ancient times. The existence of rock paintings of therianthropes (humans shape-shifting into animal form) that date back thirty-five thousand years are speculated to be the early origins of human religious traditions. The symbolic paintings and drawings on cave walls and traces of ancient rituals which appear throughout the Paleolithic Era display a 'primitive' people in touch with the unseen realm. They display a fascination with a creative world beyond that of the human reality matrix. These numerous examples of sacred, ritualistic art show how early humans were communing with a transcendental realm which modern humans have never stopped attempting to access.

Noted anthropologist David Lewis-Williams has built a theory which explains how the people of the Upper Paleolithic Era harnessed altered states of consciousness to fashion their society and used such imagery as a means of establishing and defining social relationships.[13] The rock art of shape-shifting therianthropes also suggests a 'primitive' spiritual belief in the human soul as being connected to that of an animal or another being. Here we have a clear indication of our early ancestors creating sacred ritual around the transmutation and transcending of the human, body, and mind. And this, in a nutshell, is part of the wisdom stream of shamanism (but that is another book!).

It appears then that the human body and mind have always, since the earliest known cultural records, been sites for practicing sacred transcendentalism not far off from current transhumanist notions. As a species 'in-transmutation,' we are increasingly having out-of-body experiences that meld cosmic consciousness with cultural artifacts. From the published out-of-body flights of Robert Monroe to the rise in channeled texts and audio, we have passed *beyond our senses* into a totally different multifaceted realm.* We are not wanderers in an anthropological matrix, but waves and particles in a holographic field where each flash and speck contains and reflects the whole. Enmeshed and entangled within this field matrix, we are akin to the famous Buddhist Indra's net analogy:

> Far away in the heavenly abode of the great god Indra, there is a wonderful net that has been hung by some cunning artificer in such a manner that it stretches out infinitely in all directions. In accordance with the extravagant tastes of deities, the artificer has hung a single glittering jewel in each 'eye' of the net, and since the net itself is infinite in all dimensions, the jewels are infinite in number. There hang the jewels, glittering like stars of the first magnitude, a wonderful sight to behold. If we now arbitrarily select one of these jewels for inspection and look closely at it, we will discover that in its polished surface there are reflected all the other jewels in the net, infinite in number. Not only that, but each of the jewels reflected in this one jewel is also reflecting all the other jewels, so that there is an infinite reflecting process occurring.[14]

---

*　　　See www.monroeinstitute.org for more information.

We are also reflections of ourselves in other universes as our reality matrix bends and curves throughout countless cosmic contortions. According to physicist Paul Davis, we coexist alongside countless billions of other universes 'some almost identical to ours, others wildly different, inhabited by myriads or near carbon-copies of ourselves in a gigantic, multifoliate reality of parallel worlds.'[15] We no longer know what it means to live in a dualistic subject/object type of world. Our dualistic prison walls have disintegrated around us like a simulacrum or, in more popular parlance, like a rebooting video game.

We have already passed the previous 'posts,' such as postmodernism, to arrive into a posthistoric era. Almost everything is up for grabs, which makes this era one of both spectacular possibilities as well as gravest dangers. It would appear to any off-world observer that we are in the midst of a Western slipstream of creative nihilism that is creeping its way around the fringes of tech geekiness and apocryphal, apocalyptic mysticism that says *take nothing for granted!* As the ancient mapmakers used to scribe over unknown watery territories, 'Here be dragons,' here indeed they be, like lounging lizards waiting to lick at our heels. These are adventurous times as we innovate with outer form and forge ahead into the inner spaces of essence. These are the features that adorn the sacred, the multifaceted faces of the body, mind, and environment that weave the cosmic with the social, and which collapses the wave of duality. Life 'past the post,' so to speak, is where we experiment with ourselves as a species, and as a vessel of consciousness. And this, if done in a right relationship within our reality matrix, is at its core a sacred art. As I shall endeavor to explore in the next chapter, our cultural canvas is a palimpsest upon which new fictions and artifacts are engraved. And these fictions are the channels through which the sacred revival is raising its head and smiling the seven rays of emanation.

Notes

[1] Quoted in Erik Davis, *Techgnosis: myth, magic and mysticism in the age of information* (New York: Three Rivers Press, 1998), 187.

[2] Davis, *Techgnosis*.

[3] Morris Berman, *Coming to Our Senses: Body and Spirit in the Hidden History of the West* (New York: HarperCollins, 1990).

[4] Berman, *Coming to Our Senses*, 146.

[5] William Irwin Thompson, *Coming Into Being: Artifacts and Texts in the Evolution of Consciousness* (New York: St. Martin's Griffin, 1998), 307.

[6] Thompson, *Coming Into Being*, 307.

[7] Thompson, *Coming Into Being*.

[8] Idries Shah, *The Sufis* (London: Octagon Press, 1982), 54.

[9] Timothy Leary, *Info-Psychology* (New Mexico: New Falcon Publications, 1988).

[10] Mae-Wan Ho, *The Rainbow and the Worm: The Physics of Organisms* (Singapore: World Scientific, 1998).

[11] David F. Noble, *The Religion of Technology: The Divinity of Man and the Spirit of Invention* (London: Penguin, 1999), 148-9.

[12] Juan Enriquez and Steve Gullans, *Homo Evolutis* (TED Books, 2011).

[13] David Lewis-Williams, *The Mind in the Cave: Consciousness and the Origins of Art* (London: Thames & Hudson, 2004).

[14] Quoted in Davis, *Techgnosis*, 319.

[15] Quoted in Thompson, *Coming Into Being*, 217.

6

MODERN FICTIONS:
CHAOS, SUPERHEROES, AND OUTER SPACES

The virtual topographies of our millennial world are rife with angels and aliens, with digital avatars and mystic Gaian minds, with utopian longings and gnostic science fictions, and with dark forebodings of apocalypse and demonic enchantment.
– Erik Davis, *Techgnosis*

All our so-called consciousness is a more or less fantastic commentary on an unknown, perhaps unknowable, but felt text . . .
– Frederich Nietzsche, *Daybreak: Thoughts on the Prejudices of Morality*

Science fiction is always more important than science.
– Timothy Leary, *Evolutionary Agents*

Everything that can be said has already been said, or something to that effect. It is not original to make the statement that originality no longer exists, since it's all been done before. Yet, as Marshall McLuhan famously said, 'the medium is the message.' So it may not be the message we are concerned with here, but rather the medium of its passing. And the adage goes that everything exists according to time and place. When the sacred speaks, so to speak, it does so through the ways and means of the times. This could apply to prophets, oracles, and channeling (see chapter seven) as well as pop culture and its modern fictions.

THE SACRED REVIVAL

The sacred, the sublime, has always walked among the profane. The signs are everywhere, blended into the sidewalks, pulp fictions, and the kitsch and cool of the art world. For iconic sci-fi writer Philip K. Dick, most of the sublime things of his world were disguised as trash that seamlessly slipped into the background of a dysfunctional world reality. As modern society slipstreamed into a postmodern smorgasbord of chaos, clutter, poetically burnt outbursts, and beatific revelations, a new landscape of the sacred was scattered across the bedrock. The seeming trash of the everyday mundane clashed with the incoming cosmic, and a new urge for the transcendental found its way into so many popular cultural forms that it would take an encyclopedic Möbius strip to recite it all. For my purposes here I will only briefly take a hop and skip around some of the budding flora that displayed a burgeoning sacred urge to blur the boundaries and reach for the sublime connection.

However paradoxical it may sound, one of the mediums for the sacred to spread came through the channel of chaos. Chaos, contrary to what we may think of it as being an anarchic and senseless cacophony, is actually a canvas for patterns to play out on. As the later emergence of the chaos sciences showed, there was a theory behind chaos, a method behind its apparent madness. Chaos, as we soon learned, did not operate in isolation. As the famous butterfly effect was apt at promoting, a minimal disturbance in one part of the world (e.g., a butterfly flapping its wings) could result in a climate effect in another part (a tornado was often cited). Everything thus existed in patterns and not in arbitrary, random twists and turns.

The Santa Fe Institute (founded in 1984) quickly became a prominent center for the research into complex systems, otherwise known as chaos science. Yet the emergence of chaos science had been actualized earlier through many different cultural forms of recognizing chaos as a precursor to states of consciousness. Many forms and functions that emerge as aspects of the human condition are first seeded in popular culture ahead of their wider actualization. After all, the basis of the sacred refers to actualized aspects of human consciousness. And what sacred art shows us is that its presence in our reality matrix is determined by our capacity of consciousness to receive and acknowledge it. As I discuss throughout this book, everything corresponds to our measure of consciousness. And as I shall endeavor to show in later chapters, every *form* emerges out of consciousness. Chaos, as well as 'being' patterns embedded in physical, computational, biological, and social systems, are also patterns of our minds. In fact, it can be said that chaos is part of the order of the cosmos.

THE SACRED REVIVAL

CHAOS AND THE COSMIC

' 'Tis an ill wind that blows no minds.'
— *Principia Discordia*

The signs for magic, chaos, and transcendental byways were popping up almost everywhere on the Western landscape in the postwar, postmodern years. Enochian magic, Golden Dawn rituals, and metacomputing of the self were seeding a growing experimentalism of the human mind. In the United States especially, a blend of anarchic cultural subversions were manifesting that played upon known semi-mystical memes. One of these was the text of the *Principia Discordia*, which emerged in the 1960s as a sacred text of Discordianism. Written by Malaclypse the Younger (Gregory Hill) and Omar Khayyam Ravenhurst (Kerry Thornley), it proclaimed 'All hail Discordia!' in a mixture of goddess worship with the notion of order and disorder as balancing illusions. The fifth commandment of the *Principia Discordia* states, 'A Discordian is Prohibited of Believing what he reads.'* In mode with a rising tide of memes dealing with truth through contradiction, the *Principia Discordia* also went on to claim:

---

*   Available online at http://www.sacred-texts.com/eso/pridisc.htm.

> All statements are true in some sense, false in some sense, meaningless in some sense, true and false in some sense, true and meaningless in some sense, false and meaningless in some sense, and true and false and meaningless in some sense.*

Discordia came to influence the writings of maverick author and philosopher Robert Anton Wilson, who popularized it further in his books, especially in The Illuminatus! Trilogy. These utterances were echoed by the writer William S. Burroughs who, besides experimenting in cut-up narrative techniques, proclaimed a Discordian-esque, 'Nothing is absolutely true — everything is permissible.' Burrough's infamous outburst was a culmination of religious history (the Assassins of Hassan-i Sabbah) with anarchic chaos from his spirit-possessed universe.**

Around this time literate and literary magicians were cropping up everywhere and writing tracts on magic for a modern reader. Many of these literary figures were connected to the Golden Dawn system of magic.*** Yet another emerging stream was that of chaos

---

* See http://www.sacred-texts.com/eso/pridisc.htm.
** Burroughs proclaimed that an "ugly spirit" pervaded him for his entire life, "in which I have had no choice except to write my way out." See William Burroughs: El Hombre Invisible by Barry Miles.
*** Notable figures here include Israel Regardie and Christopher S. Hyatt.

magic, which originated in United Kingdom in the late seventies. This broader magical path was liberal enough to combine forms of neoshamanism, Eastern philosophy, quantum science, visionary art, and later computer technology. This experimental perspective on magic was part of a wider trend in experimenting with known forms for new avenues of stimulating and awakening consciousness. These 'chaotic' paths were attempting to destabilize our conditioning patterns and our resultant consensus reality. They were all aimed at waking up the usually slumbering human mind. As the seminal work *Waking Up* (1986) by Charles Tart showed, humanity was largely intoxicated with a 'consensus trance' that kept us from recognizing sigils of the sacred. In more recent years the metaphors and memes of being trapped within a waking dream, or of dreams within dreams, have been explored in such popular films as *The Truman Show* (1998), the Matrix trilogy (1999-2003), and *Inception* (2010). Part of the myth we find ourselves popularizing is the mythology that we are in some sort of constructed reality, a Gnostic-inspired simulacrum of truth.

Gnostic ideas are being gnawed over, processed, and consumed in ever more popular forms of culture. There's an odd wave of mystical, spiritual impulses now radiating through popular culture that encourages us to throw ourselves into new world spaces, fantastic realms, and mythological fictions and factions. These are new mash-ups of the counterculture now being packaged and presented as part of mainstream culture. And in recent years the most extraordinary success in this area has been the incredible, phenomenal rise of the modern superhero.

SUPERHEROES AND THE SUPER-SELF

Ever since Nietzsche first declared that God is dead, we have been reeling from and dealing with our encroaching mortality — and trying to avoid this by seeking new technologies and cultural expressions of immortality. This collective experience on the possible death of god is like a sudden hammer blow that propels us against the loss of sacred meaning and sublime mystery. Whether we admit it or not, we fear the sense of absence, where nothing exists to which we can lend our communal assent. We don't wish to struggle fragmented and bewildered, abashed by creative forms of indulgence. We cannot be left behind, losing our vital contact with the imaginal, the numinous, and the magical. We cannot be left untransformed in our vacant spaces as a paranormal pop culture washes over us. No, we need our superheroes, our possibilities, our potentials. We need to find a cultural expression for the human psyche, for our psychic currents and transmissions and sacred communication. Our superheroes must live on!

Perhaps through the loss of our gods we have had to become our own gods, as we realized a need to fill a vacuum left by myth. With the loss of the godly connection, a different psychic wave was released upon the world to coincide with a rising arc of human consciousness. According to Jung: 'The gods have become diseases ... who unwittingly let loose psychic epidemics on the world.'[1] These diseases have now morphed into mutations, making us into human-god hybrids with superhuman capacities. Yet these human-god hybrids are shunned by the world for being heretical against the natural order. We have the X-Men walking amongst us, a mutant subspecies of humans.

The natural order is evo-mythological—it is sacred, beyond human, and connects us with evolutionary currents. In the absence of our ancient myths we have ingested the sacred alchemical root and through pop culture morphed this transformation into the new wave of superheroes. Myth lives anew in spandex. Maybe it is a cliché because it is true; we wish to find the personal superhero within each of us, each of our individual journeys unfolding within the great cosmic drama. This myth, this journey, has largely been taken from us through scientific rationalism and an industrial modernity. Yet now, by becoming more than oneself, we serve the larger story arc.

Our popular subcultures are gradually becoming the norm. It is not only a question of whether more people are interested or not, but rather that these ideas are more widely available now thanks to popular culture. As William Irwin Thompson notes, 'We Americans, who are so intent on creating a culture of technological materialism, cannot take in esoteric lore directly; it has to find another way in, and so comic books, science fiction, and movies are the back door.'[2]

Popular culture has been the back door for most of us, and not just for Americans. But now these back doors are merging into the background and disappearing altogether. The waking life and the dream are becoming part of the same movie plot, as in Richard Linklater's film version of Philip K. Dick's *A Scanner Darkly* (2006). We are more and more waking up into our own movie, our very own Truman Show, where ideas are seeded directly into our environments in order to catalyze our awakening. Like the tale of 'The Precious Jewel' discussed in chapter three, we have been asleep in a distant land. But now we are beginning to receive messages and signals, flashing like neon signs through our popular culture. This marks our juncture, our crisis point, between moving toward waking up or falling back into archaic, catastrophic, and catatonic slumber. Again, Thompson reminds us that we 'intuitively sense our evolutionary crisis and are expressing the catastrophe bifurcation through art — primarily through science fiction.'[3]

Our ultra high-definition visual culture is acting like a portal for the otherworld to enter. The psychedelic experiences that were once fringe and condemned are being played out again through modern fictions that blend Gnostic tropes, mythological memes, and multidimensional portholes. Transcendental states of consciousness, ratified by the far explorations of new science, are adding to the mix of a new twenty-first century mythology that as of yet remains unnamed. Our civilization is on the upward arc of human development and capacity, which, according to Sri Yukteswar, will result in enhanced mental and spiritual faculties.

Perhaps we are emerging toward the birth of new sacred gods. These are the gods of mutations, of neurological and biological adaptations. And they are emerging first in our pop culture as our superheroes and psychic mutants. In this initiation into a psychically enhanced future we will need more than ever to learn how to distinguish the demonic from the spiritual. Hence, the current barrage of cultural tropes that show angels vs. devils, humans vs. vampires, and the whole gamut of good vs. evil. All the while the Fisher King sits immobilized, feasting on an orgy of massively multiplayer online role-playing games (MMORPG). In this way the gods will never be forgotten as they merge with a super-augmented mutant humanity in spandex. As psychologist James Hillman says:

> Remember: what the Greeks said their Gods asked for above all else, and perhaps only, was not blood; it was not to be forgotten, that is, to be kept in mind, recollected as *psychological facts*. . . . [The gods'] reality can never fade as long as they are remembered, that is, kept in *mind*. That's how they survive.[4]

The real gods, as we knew all along and yet had forgotten reside within our psyche; they are kept in *mind*. And yet they can only become real for us, to re*mind* us, when dashing about on the movie screen in front of our very eyes. We need the sacred to slap our faces in spandex gloves before we begin to blink a waking eye.

As Jeffrey J. Kripal writes in his *Mutants and Mystics*, we have entered the stage of realization whereby we begin to recognize that the events around us in popular culture are not only real but participatory. That is, our sacred and supernatural fictions appear *for us* and require our engaged reading of them in order for them to read *us*. Kripal says:

> In some fundamental way that we do not yet understand, they *are* us, projected into the objective world of events and things, usually through some story, symbol, or sign. Realization is the insight that we are caught in such a story. Realization is the insight that we are being written.[5]

The latest revival in the superhero genre is significant in how it takes the mutant trope further and projects it forward as a form of evolutionary mysticism. Our new heroes are displaying to us our latent capacities and powers that are yet to unfold. We are witness to the first wave of mutant evolutionary pioneers. The summit of human evolution is far in the distance, and yet its early stages are manifesting through the Marvel and DC universes where godlike potentials await us. Through such characters as Spider-Man, Iron Man, Captain America, Wolverine, and Doctor Strange, Marvel mesmerizes paranormal subliminals into popular cultural consciousness. And DC does the same with Superman, Batman, Wonder Woman, Green Lantern, Flash, and Green Arrow. Then as gangs they come together as the Guardians of the Galaxy, the Fantastic Four, the X-Men (Marvel), or as the Justice League (DC). They are now our teachers, our guides, our mutant futures that are *beyond human*. As Kripal recognized, the mutants have become practicing mystics.

We are seemingly living more and more in a mutational and metaphysical universe, and with the arrival of augmented reality, our boundaries of interaction with the physical world around us will blur. This, as I have mentioned previously, suggests a return to the sacred perspective whereby the tangible and intangible worlds become an integral part of our holistic reality matrix. And we are already well on our way as our outer and inner spaces explode into new, blistering supernova.

OUTER SPACES AND INNER SPACES

Humankind has always been a child of the stars. Our early civilizations mapped the heavens before they mapped the terrain under their feet. The abode of the gods was among the shimmering stars of the night sky, and their chariots blazed across the incandescent cosmic canvas. So it was no surprise then when UFOs started to dart across our urban skies and come crashing down disguised as government weather balloons. Recent popular culture has nurtured a fascination with outer space and our galactic cousins from the Golden Age of Science Fiction. The concerns of our outer space relations shifted from how to make contact with our space cousins to the entropic death of the universe. And then the environmental theme and its motifs entered into perspective, as if a subliminal projection from our very own inner spaces. The sacred inner space and cosmic outer space were now aligning in their messages of concern for the future of humankind. The growing number of alleged UFO abductees that emerged in the latter part of the twentieth century began to relay messages of extraterrestrial concern for our planetary well-being.

John E. Mack, who was an American professor of psychiatry at Harvard Medical School, became a leading authority on the spiritual or transformational effects of the alien abduction experience. Mack came to view the alien abduction phenomenon as acting as a catalyst to 'shatter the boundaries of the psyche and to open consciousness to a wider sense of existence and connection in the universe.'[6] For more than a decade Mack rigorously studied the alien abduction phenomenon and interviewed hundreds of people (whom Mack referred to as 'experiencers'). What initially started out as an exercise in studying mental illness soon turned into an in-depth inquiry into personal and spiritual transformation.

Mack eventually came to see the alien abduction phenomenon as one of the most powerful agents for spiritual growth, personal transformation, and expanded awareness. In other words, as a trigger for a sacred experience. Despite the external anxiety produced by the experience, it was clear to both Mack and his set of experiencers that a profound communion was being established between humankind and other realities. Further, that this interaction was catalyzing a shift in human consciousness toward collapsing the old models of materialistic duality and opening up a connection not only beyond the Earth, but with other dimensional realities. Mack notes that 'the process of psychospiritual opening that the abduction phenomenon provokes may bring experiencers to a still deeper level of consciousness where the oneness or interconnectedness of creation becomes a compelling reality.'[7]

This interconnectedness became a channel for the experiencers (abductees) to receive an impressive range of information, such as healing knowledge, spiritual truths, science, technology, and ecology. A major part of the information was apparently concerning the status of the Earth and humanity's relationship with its environment. Many of the experiencers referred to their own abduction phenomenon as participating in a transdimensional or interspecies relationship. The transformative effects of these unusual encounters were often remarkable. Mack's experiencers talked about an expansion of psychic or intuitive abilities, a heightened reverence for nature, the feeling of having a special mission on Earth, the collapse of space/time perception, an understanding of the multidimensions of reality and the existence of multiverses, a feeling of connection with all of creation, and a whole range of related transpersonal experiences.

Significant from these accounts is that, according to the experiencers, the abduction phenomenon is sometimes accompanied by a sense of moving into, or connecting with, other realities or dimensions. The sacred space and outer space were becoming one and the same. Or to put it another way, the contact initiated from those 'out there' was having a catalyzing effect, triggering an awakening in the inner spaces way 'down here.' It made sense then that our human future was going to include space migration. And according to our galactic cousins, it may even be a necessity if we continued to destroy our planetary home.

Inner space junkie Timothy Leary was already riding that space-me-outta-here ticket with his SMI^{2}LE philosophy. Leary's SMI^{2}LE stood for Space Migration, Increased Intelligence, and Life Extension. Basically, these were all the tropes from the posthumanism mélange added on to the sci-fi dream of humanity living off-planet. We also now have the commercial race to establish a new branch of space tourism, with Virgin Galactic being one of the visible and vocal frontrunners. SpaceX, another private enterprise, is banking its dollars on helping to colonize Mars. There's no lack of vision, it's now down to the know-how and the technological leg up.

Now that the space cat is out the bag (excuse the pun), it's only a matter of time before the picture we have of being human will incorporate the starry, cold vistas of outer space. From the earliest sacred expressions in the cave art of our ancestors to the ideas of space migration, two fundamental urges within human beings are apparent: 1) I am human, I am here (recognition); and 2) Where is the heavenly connection? (contact). Human dreams have encompassed living on Mars, leaving and migrating beyond the solar system, and of contact with a 'higher intelligence.'

Gene Roddenberry, creator of *Star Trek*, managed to combine both contact and communication through his receiving of channeled information. It has been documented that Roddenberry was introduced to an entity called Tom, who represented the Council of Nine, through the channel medium Phyllis Schlemmer. Roddenberry was allegedly receiving information for a film script to be written that would help prepare the public for extraterrestrial contact. The alleged film never got made, yet we might wonder what ideas made their way into *Star Trek* (including *Star Trek: Deep Space Nine*). It appears that there are those 'out there' who are concerned for our proper preparation for the sacred communion. And the archetypes are now flooding through our popular culture like an evangelical tsunami.

The mythic archetypes from Joseph Campbell's *The Hero with a Thousand Faces* filled out the roles in George Lucas's epic Star Wars universe. The good, the bad, and the hairy all took their cue and played along with the hero's journey for an updated mythological rendering. While the rise of industrial modernity and the secularization of culture may have contributed to an eroding of our myth consciousness and a demotion of mystery, a new vital force has emerged that is shifting our planetary pranic energy. There may be those who bemoan that our current civilization does not have a mythic center, yet they're missing the point. And this point is that there is no exact *point* anymore. As Hermetic lore states, the center is everywhere and the circumference nowhere. The earlier gods retreated back on their sky chariots until we finally had to ask ourselves where they all went. The new sacred guides are now secreted in our popular texts that penetrate our outer and inner worlds. These posthistoric mythic guides are first to be found within us, within our collective species psyche, which gets projected out onto our celluloid and digital landscapes. These remodeled, mythic memes are telling us that we are not here alone, nor are we here for ourselves alone. The future is not only arriving, it is here now, and has already been.

We have such films as *Back to the Future*, *Primer*, *Looper*, *Terminator*, *Interstellar*, and all the rest to attest to our obsession with shifting our time-oriented perspectives. Everything is now malleable, according to our new quantum sciences, and our sacred revival is knocking down linear walls of rigidity. Just when you thought that you were safe in stable comfort zones, the paranormal is getting ready to redress itself as the new normal. A Gnostic-like awareness of being embedded in a reality construct will become ever greater as our technologies increasingly broker and interface our physical experience. There are a plentiful array of fictions and films that ply us with plots on technologically-driven machine gnosis. Perhaps they are trying to signal that we are entering the sacred space of hybrid awareness. The film *Transcendence* (2014), for example, showed humanity edging toward sacred sentience as a means for solving the world's global problems. As Václev Havel stated in one of his addresses, 'Transcendence is the only real alternative to extinction.' Yet we are not on our way out, despite what the fearmongering mainstream media may be trying to ram down our throats. Nor are we heading toward a techno-machine overlord future with us as the slaves. This is because the sacred works in multiple streams and never hedges all bets on a one-trick pony.

  The game changer coming onto the scene is the participatory mind of human consciousness. The coming space migration is a reflection of our expanding inner spaces. We are toying with these memes in our popular culture before their coming actualization. What our fictions are dealing with are the blueprints before we're ready to go the whole hog. And that's why we're in a period of incredible experimentation. We are juggling with a new type of energy coming into our cultural realities. And this new pranic force is getting expressed in a myriad of multiple forms, be it creatively, chaotically, commercially, or crazily. It's a cacophony of exuberance and experimentation trying to find its harmonic resonance. We are gaming, bopping, and trailblazing our way into a re-identification with a sacred perspective. And it is from this springboard where we dive into the next chapter filled with ecstatic highs, techno-trance, and digital Gnostics.

Notes

[1] Sabini, *C. G. Jung on Nature, Technology & Modern Life*, 98.

[2] Thompson, *Coming Into Being*, 218.

[3] Thompson, *Coming Into Being*, 223.

[4] Hollis, *Tracking the Gods*, 147.

[5] Jeffrey J. Kripal, *Mutants & Mystics: Science Fiction, Superhero Comics, and the Paranormal* (Chicago: The University of Chicago Press, 2011), 217-18.

⁶ John, E. Mack, *Passport to the Cosmos: Human Transformation & Alien Encounters* (New York: Crown Publishers, 1999), 218.

⁷ Mack, *Passport to the Cosmos*, 136.

7

NEON TRIBES: ECSTATIC HIGHS, TECHNO-TRANCE, AND DIGITAL GNOSTICS

There are people in the world all the time who know. . . . But they keep quiet. They just move about quietly, saving the people who know they are in the trap. And then, for the ones who have got out, it's like coming around from chloroform. They realize that all their lives they've been asleep and dreaming. And then it's their turn to learn the rules and the timing. And they become the ones to live quietly in the world, just as human beings might if there were only a few human beings on a planet that had monkeys on it for inhabitants, but the monkeys had the possibility of learning to think like human beings. But in the poor sad monkeys' damaged brains there's a knowledge half-buried. They sometimes think that if they only knew how, if only they could remember properly, then they could get out of the trap, they could stop being zombies. It's something like that.
— Doris Lessing, Briefing for a Descent into Hell

Students achieving Oneness will move on to Twoness.
— Woody Allen

Coming around from chloroform is an apt analogy for some of what is going on right now. Our new cultures are re-forming after their postmodernity heyday of scrambled identities and loss of metanarratives. Things fall apart in order to come back together. While William Irwin Thompson remarks that, 'Our new culture is not so much postmodern as postcivilized . . . an electronic meltdown of civilization in which barbarism and savagery boil up to the surface once again,' what is boiling up is a different kind of savagery.[1] Sure, there are the usual shenanigans going on all over the world thanks largely to our fossilized political institutions, yet an altogether diverse dynamic is boiling up through our electronic melting pot.

The media theorist Marshall McLuhan noted that we are passing through an era that will require a need to gather up the broken fragments of a retribalized humanity. And that is the sense that hits us, as if the emerging global spaces are retribalizing us 'out of the trees and into history,' and re-forming the species as a global tribe, all neon-lit for a new technologically assisted reality set.[2] As a species we have changed dramatically over the preceding epochs. As Terence McKenna notes:

> We are no longer bipedal monkeys. We are instead a kind of cybernetic coral reef of organic components and inorganic technological components. We have become a force that takes unorganized raw material and excretes technical objects; we have transcended the normal definitions of humans. We are like an enormous collective organism with our data banks, our forecasting agencies, and our computer networks, and the many levels at which we are connected into the universe. Our self-image is changing; the monkey has been all but left behind and, shortly, *will* be left behind.[3]

The new tribal cult is now morphing into the early birth pangs of a planetary civilization. The monkey mind is fading into obsolescence, although its aged adherents cling on desperately for their final gasps of air. This is the bifurcation point where we leap into the fiery cultural furnace to forge a new species consciousness, or wrangle with the old like an asphyxiated puppy. In the words of Thompson, we either 'shift upward to a new culture of a higher spirituality to turn our electronic technologies into cathedrals of light, or we slide downward to darkness and entropy in a war of each against all.'[4]

This is the current medley we are dancing with, and yet I cannot personally see this sliding downward into an entropic darkness. The possibility is there for sure, and has always been there, and yet the energy is perhaps too dynamic now to allow for a downbeat or dead rhythm. And so I see the 'cathedrals of light' being the more likely option, though it won't be an overnight construction. The great cathedral builders of old did not accomplish their masonic texts so easily. We are still attempting to bebop alongside the 'droning Muzak inside an electropop mediocracy.'[5] The neon tribes of the digital age are seeking alternative spiritual streams, and yet the search for ecstatic highs within the inner landscape are fraught with frauds and superficial vendors. The marketplace has never been as full as it is now, nor as diverse and tantalizing.

ECSTATIC HIGHS

The sacred revival has its counterparts and copycats; its true gold is mixed in with the false gold. A spiritual marketplace has arisen to satisfy (or con) the needs of the hungry awakeners. Gurus have cropped up, both indigenous and imported, to sprinkle the fairy dust of magical inducements and Samadhic temptations. And not just for the inner world either. People are now grooming themselves as social media gurus ready to offer guidance for the digital byways. Life coaching is also a relatively new term and profession, offering assistance for those seeking clarity in their oh-so fuzzy lives. And did you know that life coaches claim you can earn high five- to six-figure salaries from life coaching?

As with anything, when a new idea, form, or energy emerges into the physical world, it soon gives birth to a range of appropriated offspring. Some of these forms become crystallized, such as in dogmatic belief systems, while others get commercialized, such as in the sweatbox of New Age swagger. The range and diversity of popular culture (especially Westernized cultural forms) include the eclectic, consumerist, and commercial that offer a plethora of choices in the belief that more is better. This encourages some people to experiment, taste, and dabble with a ragbag of spiritual goodies in the hope that the resulting fusion will do some good.

Sometimes it is the case that people wish to receive 'of the spirit' in accordance to what they imagine spirituality to be. The following anecdote serves as an example of this. A visitor to a spiritual order, upon being received by the revered spiritual sheikh, suggested that the practices he was advocating belonged to a time in the past and were limited for a specific, targeted audience. Since such conditions no longer existed, the visitor pointed out, then what remained was merely an outer core, a spectacle. The old sheikh, who was the head of the order, replied:

> I have been here so long, and so have my ancestors, that we cannot change. . . . We may well be wanted, and believed to be the possessors of secrets. . . . We are here, after seven hundred years, not because of our value or viciousness, but because people *want* us. They want magic. . . . Many can follow a harmless path and feel better, elevated. That, in any case, is what they imagine spirituality to be.[6]

Popular culture has a great way of taking various forms and practices and utilizing them to reinforce mental, emotional, and physical conditioning and patterns of behavior. It's all part of what we'll call the 'one hundred aspirin effect,' whereby we miscalculate the dosage of something merely because we believe that more of a good thing will only bring us more good. But while taking an aspirin for a headache can do a lot of good, taking a hundred would have an adverse effect and could even kill you.

THE SACRED REVIVAL

The 'post-something' stage we are currently riding—whether it be postmodernity or posthistoric—is bound to reify desires and urges into cultural totems for consumption. It's all part of the flux, flotsam, and flow that goes with cultural trends. What's significant about the present cultural candy store is that it has increasingly come to be dominated by spiritual and transformative memes. Quotations and phrases for inner transformation and well-being—once the tropes of Delphic maxims and prophetic pronouncements—are now slapped around as social media sound bites and Facebook photos. Anyone with a computer and free photo editing software can now mix and match their feel-good totems in the transcendental marketplace. The counterfeit exists because the 'real' is out there, and the superficial pronouncements only strengthen the fact that the sacred, which is a science of transformation, is now emerging through the common cultural sphere. What was once the purview, the secret domain, of the mystery schools is now seeping into mass circulation. This denotes that a particular stage of mass consciousness is coming into effect. The impulse to transcend—the Neoplatonist ascent, the Gnostic awakening through the illusion, the rejection of monkish, cave dweller activity—all point toward an internal longing now being played out in the tribal fields of a new spiritual smorgasbord.

Selling the supernatural has never been so lucrative. The Wal-Marts of America are now offering a well-stocked 'gateway to a strange world of supernatural living and suburban sorcery,' which forms 'a full scale assault on the American mindscape.'[7] A paranormal pop culture is now the norm, as esoteric streams seep into mass consciousness through spandex-clad mutants or cleverly woven sci-fi stories. The occult is no longer hidden, but openly gallops through our living rooms through the new expansive digital byways that entrain our minds through the guise of entertainment. The new neon tribes of a digitally-enhanced world are responding to an altered sensorial reality set. For the young generations especially, a new experience is being sought and longed for because they have been born into a different sensory environment. As media theorist Marshall McLuhan identified as far back as the 1960s, new cultural technology 'inevitably creates new environments that act incessantly on the sensorium.'[8] We will experience new sensations as we try to adjust to the emerging sensory environments created by the global digital technologies that McLuhan rightly identified as being extensions of our own nervous system.

Furthermore, as our current civilization shifts and gets remade under the digitalizing revolution, 'we discover a tribal, integral awareness that manifests itself in a complete shift in our sensory lives' as 'a resonating world akin to the old tribal echo chamber where magic will live again.'[9] As the digital-physical merger increasingly unfolds through our reality, new forms of retribalization may emerge through a range of mediums. Various forms of the participatory mystique and group identification have exploded through online networks, forums, chat groups, video conferencing, and so forth. The chaos magicians (introduced in chapter six) have even appropriated the digital realms for the simulation of the online ritual environment as they perform together through video streaming. And yet these re-formations are not only digital or anti-physical, but are also resacralizing the energy of meetingness. That is, they are reverting to physical and community gatherings. As a rebellious affront to the hierarchical corporate world of modernity, the neopagan neon tribes of sacralized individuals are conjuring up their own carnivals and field gatherings. Within this 'horizontal zone of becoming . . . the center is always decentered. . . . The carnival fragments and distributes the power that the ladder concentrated into one supreme point. Nature speaks again, in a thousand networked tongues.'[10]

In recent years carnivals and art and music festivals have been springing up all over the globe. Some of these festivals of play and enactment are like a medieval mirror to the Rabelaisian world of ribaldry and protest. The continuation of this medieval outburst can be witnessed in southern Spain's Andalusia province. The Andalusian capital, Cádiz, continues to host the lengthy carnivals of a folk culture filled with outrage, sociopolitical angst, and ecstatic partying along with songs and merry indulgence. These carnivals are mirrored in various towns dotted throughout the Andalusian landscape. Yet now these localized tribal merriments have gone global as the digitally-infused neon tribes of today are delving into trance, techno, burning art, and muddy fields.

TRIBAL MEETINGNESS AND TECHNO-TRANCE

From Glastonbury to Goa, the carnival co-opts nature into a raving fusion of music, energy, vibe, and exuberant dance—a glocal tribal meetingness.* The Glastonbury Festival, which began in a Somerset field in the United Kingdom in 1970, is a five-day festival of contemporary performing arts that includes music, theatre, comedy, circus, cabaret, and other acts, some of which are spontaneous. It is now the largest open-field festival in the world and attracts around 175,000 people. It is also famous not only for its megastar music performers but also for its notorious rain and muddy fields. Yet this seems to deter no one, as festival goers revel in mud-caked glory to the vibes that flow from the Pyramid stage to the circus, from Left field to the Glade. There are art installations and debates, dance trances and good old rock 'n' roll. It is a Gnostic pageant, a witchery of gatherings, a kaleidoscopic meeting of exuberant individuals that is seen all over in other similar festivals such as Roskilde, Boom, Burning Man, Newport, Isle of Wight, and literally hundreds more.

One of the precursors to these sacred tribalizations was the Woodstock festival, a three-day festival in

August 1969 that attracted an estimated attendance of 400,000 people. A year later, the 1970 Isle of Wight festival was said at the time to have been one of the largest human gatherings in the world, with estimates of over 600,000 people. In the last two decades especially, the festival scene has been revived to an unprecedented level, aided by exposure through digital media.

Similarly, the Burning Man festival, held in the Black Rock Desert in Nevada in the United States, is a community gathering of self-expression, art, architecture, exhibition, and exploration. Burning Man is about collage and juxtaposition — a post-postmodern mélange of meshing collaborations that is a visual and aural feast. It is a public art house with no walls or roof, and plays with the disenchantment of an industrial modernity, recasting it into an alien landscape. Some may say it bears a similarity to the Eleusinian Mysteries, the greatest known public cult gathering of ancient Greece, where people took initiatory processions through the streets. Larry Harvey, one of the founders of Burning Man, has himself noted that the Nevada festival, like the Mysteries, attracts a largely urban and sophisticated crowd, unlike some of the musical festival goers. Harvey feels that Burning Man is more about inward feelings than exuberant emotional release.

Erik Davis, a US cultural journalist who has attended several Burning Man events, calls it 'a promiscuous carnival of souls, a metaphysical flea market, a demolition derby of reality constructs colliding in a parched void.'[11] At the core of the Burning Man immersion is the cult of experience. As cofounder Larry Harvey says, 'Beyond belief, beyond the dogmas, creeds, and metaphysical ideas of religion, there is immediate experience.'[12] As in other wisdom traditions, the aim is not in doctrinal rules but in practical means for changing consciousness. As in tribal initiations, experience is the real teacher, a ritual process that can forge a new mode of social being. Such gatherings as those mentioned can provide a space for transformative experiences, for unexpected happenings to occur that can trigger episodes of meaning. Such carnivals, festivals, and physical gatherings hold no overt claims for power or significance. Rather, they offer a space for creative intensity, for a new tribal sensorium or 'carnival of consciousness' (to quote Davis) that celebrates the human visionary capacity. The rise in such festivals represents a sacred colonization, a retribalization, of a static space in the ordinary world that then dissolves back after its high-spirited outburst. After Burning Man, the Nevada desert goes back to its drifting sands; after Glastonbury the fields return to grass waving in the breeze. Yet for a short moment of creative intensity these spaces play out a sacred tribal reenactment that affects the human consciousness.

In a way this is similar to how the ancient Mystery initiations — and the archaic minds of our ancestral cave painters — entered into transcendental states. Such festivals open up what Hakim Bey has called 'temporary autonomous zones,' or uprisings of energy and ecstasy that merge emotions with euphoria and delight, contorting the waves of consciousness. They display a powerful assemblage of social, human, and creative forces that pierce against the bubble of protective reality and seek to take a peek outside of our collective dream. They show us a glimpse that, through each waking moment, we are experiencing a dissolution and reenactment of the world, a reflection of our bardo lives. In these moments, we experience the trance within the trance that is our transitory state.

Such states of trance are also well known to the Goa music subcultures that grew up in Goa, India, in the seventies and eighties. The now famous Goa trance music scene grew out of the all-night music parties on the beaches of Goa. At the time, imported music on tapes and MIDIs were sampled by resident hippie DJs, as well as visiting DJs. The scene was initially below the radar until it became globally known in the nineties, by which time it attracted trance enthusiasts the world over.

The early Goa crowd were often called 'cyber hippies' for their infusion of techno music sounds and equipment (synthesizer and electronic sounds and mixing desks) combined with Eastern mysticism and psychedelic culture. Goa Gil, an American-born musician who was one of the early Goa trance DJs, described his role by saying, 'I'm basically just using this whole party situation as a medium to do magic, to remake the tribal pagan ritual for the twenty-first century.'[13] Goa Gil, through the trance-haze of his mind, is sharp enough to recognize exactly where this sacred music fest is located — a magical 'tribal pagan ritual for the twenty-first century.' Similarly, another Goa trance musician, Raja Ram, when interviewed by Erik Davis about his music, said: 'You have to become a neuronaut to understand this music. We've gone from flint-rock to the moon landing in a few thousand years, and now we're on the edge of the world opened up with information machines. This is a new inner space we're exploring.'[14]

The Goa scene was a physical location exploited for exploring the inner space through a merging of machine technology with electronic beats and swirls — the perfect collusion for the sacred vibe to be seeded. It marked a journey of modernity from the ecstatic religious dervish dancing of India to the interstellar trance beats of a cyber, techno-trance imported influx from the Western shores. European hipsters descended into Goa wearing sneakers and flared jeans as an escape from the corporate world of industrial consciousness. They trance-swirled and gyrated through their opening inner landscapes in a desire for a small grasp of the celestial firmament. As Davis aptly describes it:

> These melodies and beats are created, recorded, and reproduced in the digital ether of electronic circuitry. ... These transient refugees from the First World have poached the info tech that's speeding up the march of progress and made an abrupt about-face towards the archaic. ... Technology loves connection, so they sync it with the ancient wheel of the heavens.[15]

This represents one aspect of the emergent energy and consciousness that belongs to the burgeoning sacred revival. It shows how technology is merging with a new vibration (music) to sacralize a part of the human consciousness (inner spaces) that had hitherto remained suppressed. It is the Mozart for the new millennium. And this combination of external and internal technologies is all meshed with what can be termed as the digital Gnostics.

DIGITAL GNOSTICS

As I touched on earlier, the late twentieth century saw an explosion in countercultural spirituality. As part of the emerging experimental playscape there arose an assortment of techniques, from kundalini-catalyzing yoga to psychedelic pseudo-shamanic head trips. A plethora of new spiritual and sacred techniques filled the consumerist seeker's shopping basket, what Mircea Eliade, a Romanian historian of religion, referred to as 'techniques of ecstasy.' These techniques later began to combine with the new 'machine vocabulary' to produce such systems as 'metaprogramming the human biocomputer.' This new affinity for digitally inspired transcendence marked the arrival of a 'sacred mechanics' that merged the machine with the sacred. It seemed to be no mere accident that many of the spiritual advocates who venerated the old codes of the sacred were now embracing the new programs offered by technology.

A high percentage of self-confessed modern pagans, when surveyed by reporter and fellow pagan Margot Adler in her work *Drawing Down the Moon: Witches, Druids, Goddess-Worshippers, and Other Pagans in America*, were found to be involved in computer and technology fields. Modern pagans were also, it seemed, adept video gamers. The stream had flowed from the witches circles of old to the new digital spaces of sorcery in virtual circles. There is little doubt that a digital culture exists that thrives on neo-paganism and a mix of the magical and the mystical.

A thorough survey of this eclectic space was eloquently expounded by Erik Davis in his classic work *TechGnosis: Myth, Magic, and Mysticism in the Age of Information* (1998). The spirit now appears to be infusing our playful pastimes in the virtual domain. You could wander through an excess of video games now on the market and many of them would convey Gnostic or sacred themes. Apart from the obvious Matrix video games, other similar examples include the Final Fantasy franchise, the Xenogears and Xenosago series, *Ghost in the Shell: First Assault*, and countless others that are beyond the scope of this brief foray.

The notion of self-transcendence in a reality construct is ideally suited to the format of the virtual world of video gaming. As Davis notes, 'Gnosticism creates a space to step back and critique the dominant situation, a space of visionary alienation that reveals the cracks in the surface of apparent reality.'[16] Video gaming puts the gamer in the center of this apparent reality from which they are challenged to explore, prevail, attain, and ascend. Gamers participate with their realities—they are not simply observers. This elevates the partnership into the transcendent realm of play.

Both our physical, external reality and our gaming realities are closely entwined in a fortuitous web. The latest in scientific research—our quantum sciences where perceived reality is 'collapsed into being' from observation—reveals a Gnostic tinge to what we consider to be reality. In the virtual gaming worlds our gods are challenged, and often found to be lacking. They are the Gnostic demiurges that try to throw a veil over our understanding. These demiurges are like the never seen game designer, whose design plans are carefully and creatively hidden within the gameplay. To reveal the plans of the designer, or creator, could potentially spoil the game, or create a shortcut to its end goal and destiny. Gamers keep a close attention upon the signs and clues in the game in the hope of figuring out the built-in road map. This is similar to how kabbalists sought the secret hidden in knowable patterns of numbers and letters. Our digital topographies 'are rife with angels and aliens, with digital avatars and mystic Gaian minds, with utopian longings and Gnostic science fictions, and with dark forebodings of apocalypse and demonic enchantment.'[17]

In such digital spaces we are often urged to become our own gods through trial and error, or through augmentation of our digital 'selves.' In the words of philosopher Michael Heim, 'What better way to emulate God's knowledge than to generate a virtual world constituted by bits of information. Over such a cyber world human beings could enjoy a godlike instant access.'[18] Through such demiurge access we can upgrade our bodies and minds in order to overcome adversities, or experiment time and again like some reincarnating cycle. Gamers believe that they have free will and intention as they move through the narrative gameplay, accepting the consequences to their actions. They deny the artifice of the reality in which they are immersed. The original sin of video games, according to gaming scholar Liel Leibovitz, is 'reminding players that they're nothing but pawns in a hermetically sealed universe crafted by an unknown creator, playing by rules they will never entirely understand.'[19]

Despite some of the criticism thrown at video games (for example, their depiction of violence), many games offer a platform for mystical, philosophical inquiry, cognitive puzzles, creative problem-solving, and imaginative world building. It is little wonder then that the technology industry is filled with science fiction fans and fantasy geeks who cut their teeth on masters like Isaac Asimov and Arthur C. Clarke, as well as the philosophies of Pierre Teilhard de Chardin. There is something inherently sacred and spiritual about our technologies of connection and communication.

Notes

[1] Thompson, *Coming Into Being*, 1.

[2] McKenna, *The Archaic Revival*, 167.

[3] McKenna, *The Archaic Revival*, 166.

[4] Thompson, *Coming Into Being*, 10.

[5] Thompson, *Coming Into Being*, 2.

[6] John Grant, *Travels in the Unknown East* (London: Octagon Press, 1992), 43.

[7] David Metcalfe, 'Satan's Target: Your Mind—Supernatural Living in the American Marketplace,' *United Academics Journal of Social Sciences* Vol. 3 Issue 17 (2013).

[8] Marshall McLuhan and Quentin Fiore, *War and Peace in the Global Village* (New York: Bantam Books, 1968), 136.

[9] McLuhan and Fiore, *War and Peace in the Global Village*, 24.

[10] Erik Davis, *Nomad Codes: Adventures in Modern Esoterica* (Portland, OR: Verse Chorus Press, 2010), 160.

[11] Davis, *Nomad Codes*, 317.

[12] Quoted in Davis, *Nomad Codes*, 320.

[13] Quoted in Davis, *Nomad Codes*, 52.

[14] Quoted in Davis, *Nomad Codes*, 48.

[15] Davis, *Nomad Codes*, 58.

[16] Davis, *Nomad Codes*, 157.

[17] Davis, *Techgnosis*, 5.

[18] Quoted in Noble, *The Religion of Technology*, 159.

[19] Liel Leibovitz, *God in the Machine: Video Games as Spiritual Pursuit* (West Conshohocken, PA: Templeton Press, 2013), 14.

8

I SCRATCH YOUR BACK, YOU SCRATCH MINE: A NEW COMMUNION IN COMMUNICATION

In the five-billion-year history of our planet, written literacy is less than an eye blink.
– David Fideler, Restoring the Soul of the World

The aspiration of our time for wholeness, empathy, and depth of awareness is a natural adjunct of electronic technology.
– Marshal McLuhan, Understanding Media

Language is everything. Language is a code that programs our communication. Yet it also serves to decode incoming information. That is, the language we use filters and interprets our specific cultural reality. It is a powerful tool. Perhaps that is why literacy—language through text—was once a skill kept only for an elite minority. It was guarded as a sacred tool, regarded as an initiation, and held secret from the masses. Literacy gave access to knowledge and opened up channels to the divine. Protecting it gave great power to its holders. Unleashing it changed human society beyond measure.

As cultural historian Walter Ong remarked, 'More than any other single invention, writing has transformed human consciousness.'[1] Throughout human history, each new way of communicating has catalyzed a shift in how people perceive reality. From the alphabet to the printing press, the telegraph to the telephone, and the television to the computer, each phase has profoundly transformed our modes of civilization. Each form of a communication technology, each with its own mode of transmission, insinuates itself into the collective psyche of the society which uses them, and once embedded begins to influence and reshape cultural perceptions. Media ecologist Robert K. Logan notes:

> A medium of communication is not merely a passive conduit for the transmission of information but rather an active force in creating new social patterns and new perceptual realities. A person who is literate has a different world view than one who receives information exclusively through oral communication. The alphabet, independent of the spoken languages it transcribes or the information it makes available, has its own intrinsic impacts.[2]

For example, how a child learns to perceive and integrate the cultural information from its environment will play a role in determining which neuronal pathways of their developing brain will be reinforced. This mental and emotional formation has been occurring to human beings in many ways, both religious and social, through the ages.

I SCRATCH YOUR BACK, YOU SCRATCH MINE

Liturgical murmurs, religious chants, sacred mantras, bodily mimetic gestures, mnemonic invocations, and uttered intentions are all forms of language, expression, and influence. They are all forms of magic, too. Language is power. It always has been and always will be. Language is a science, a tool, a technology. It is also a form of magic through which we conjure tangible and intangible worlds, grapple with forces outside and in, and entangle ourselves, begging entry, into the cosmos's innermost mysteries. We interpret and communicate the mysteries through language, whether it be ancient rock art or mathematical equations. It may even be a look, a gesture, or a sense. Our senses are a language, and language is as much *how* we communicate something as it is the content of what we communicate. In the famous maxim of Marshall McLuhan, *the medium is the message*.

Language is everything. Language is a sense that conveys information. In the words of Terence McKenna:

> The world is made of language. Language is replicating itself in DNA, which, at the evolutionary apex, is creating societies of civilized beings that possess languages and machines that use languages. Earth is a place where language has literally become alive. Language has infested matter; it is replicating and defining and building itself. And it is in us.[3]

Language is in us. It connects us to our world and allows us to transcribe our sense of reality. Language also fosters a sense of communion with the sacred — it gives us a channel onto the *other worlds*.

CHANGING CHANNELS: ANCIENT ORACLES IN MODERN VOICES

~ Know thyself ~
~ Know what you have learned ~
~ Perceive what you have heard ~
~ If you are a stranger act like one ~
~ Control yourself ~
~ Exercise nobility of character ~

—Delphic maxims

The phenomenon known as channeling is almost as old as human civilization itself. Contrary to what people may think, it is not only a modern phenomenon related to discarnate entities, séances, or some New Age communiqué with Ashtar Command. In the early forms it was oral communications, such as those given by oracles, prophets, and seers. Channeling is one aspect of divination, depending on the source of the information.

The famous Pythia (Oracle of Delphi, established in the eight century BCE) is one known example of this. Such maxims provided by the Oracle of Delphi, as shown above, have trickled down into common usage. Who has not come across the maxim 'know thyself,' which now adorns T-shirts and bumper stickers? In its time, the communications from the Greek Pythia were mentioned by such luminaries as Aristotle, Euripides, Herodotus, Ovid, Plato, and Sophocles. These prophetic pronouncements were regarded with great importance and seriousness. In this context, only specific individuals were regarded as suitable (or clean) channels for receiving such sacred communications. Sometimes, as in the case of the Oracle of Delphi, the person was carefully selected and initiated for the coveted position. In other cases, the source chose to select the receiver.

Muhammad, the Holy Prophet of Islam, was chosen to receive the revelations from the archangel Gabriel. These revelations were later preserved as texts and formed the Quran. Language was the medium for this sacred transmission, first orally and later through script. Other religious movements were also said to have been started by receiving communications from the spirit realm, such as Mormonism, founded by the received revelations of Joseph Smith, Jr. Similarly, Bernadette Soubirous of Lourdes, France, is said to have received instructions from the apparition of the Virgin Mary in 1858. Over the centuries the medium of revelation established a communiqué that formed a language bridge between worlds. Different reality sets were connected and information communicated. This was seen as merging the profane world with the sacred. These prophetic occurrences, however, were few until recent years.

THE SACRED REVIVAL

The second half of the twentieth century saw an influx of channeled information. The most famous of these are the material of 'Seth' from Jane Roberts, *A Course in Miracles* from Helen Schucman, 'Ramtha' from JZ Knight, 'Ra' from Carla Rueckert, 'Pleiadians' from Barbara Marciniak, and many, many more. From the Oracle of Delphi to angels and extraterrestrial intelligences, we've just been changing channels.

The gods may have left us, yet they always kept the communication channels open. It seems we are unable to ignore the sacred transmissions. They speak to us through the psyche, which we then project through our own mediums of communication, with images and symbolism. Initially the few receivers of such information were constricted by an oral tradition. Their advice and maxims were spread by word of mouth, or etched into signs and hung above doorways. Then later, through script and text, they traveled further afield to infect peoples' minds. Viruses of sacred transmission were invading the minds of humanity through various streams, both religious and secular. Then human intellect came along and rationally tried to divorce such sacred transmissions from our reality and deny them their existence within our psyches. They were proclaimed as either religious revelations or the rantings of a lunatic, and so the profane and the sacred were separated.

Then popular culture and mass communications arrived to once again provide a steady stream for a sacred communion. Right on time it seemed. Our reality was blown wide open by the mass arrival of new programming riding on the back of easily transmitted language: 'Reality is truly a creature made of language and of linguistic structures that you carry, unbeknown to yourself.'[4] The new programming for our reality is being transmitted through our expanding communications media. We have allowed a new form of nervous system to emerge, creeping across the surface of our world, carving out its channels. These channels are the new digital topographies that sculpt the human consciousness.

DIGITAL TOPOGRAPHIES: FROM LOGOS TO LOGO

For both Marshall McLuhan and Jean Gebser, the evolution of folk society into literate civilization is marked by an increasing visualization of consciousness. When alphabetic print suddenly emerged into Western culture, it brought with it an individualizing effect. After all, reading and writing is a solitary endeavor. The act of reading a book generates beta waves, which is associated with active thinking, and stimulates the left side of the brain. Visual digital media like television, on the other hand, activates the right side of the brain. So it is not only the content that is important, but the process of receiving the information and how it reconfigures the brain and affects our perception of reality. Remember, the medium is the message!

The use of the keyboard has transformed mainly right-hand writing (left brain) into simultaneous dexterous hand movement utilizing both sides of the brain. Then the mouse and cursor arrived, which uses hand-eye coordination that is more spatial than linear. 'The mouse scurries across the corpus callosum, and invites right-brain pattern skills to participate in the manoeuvres necessary to generate the written word.'[5] At each step our technologies take us toward the communal, creative, and imaginative space. Literacy, alongside the image and iconic communication, can help to bring both hemispheres into balance. Now, however, it appears that the image — the original medium of the sacred — is coming back into vogue, with a counterblast.

While written texts took five centuries to permeate world culture, television managed the same penetration in only five decades, and the computer (and Internet) has achieved this in only one decade. Our modern popular cultures are now visual landscapes, dripping in icons. The classical Greek *logos* meant 'the word,' and now in the new millennium of the twenty-first century, it has contracted to become *logo*, the icon. As part of our transition to the emerging digital topographies, we are witnessing a rebalancing of *logos* and *logo,* and a revival of the imaginal realm.

James Burke and Robert Ornstein, in their cultural study on innovation, suggest that our highly visual culture of multimedia icons, multitasking, and digital spaces will resurrect our earlier 'magical' mode of consciousness based on intuition, imagination, and the spatial.[6] The image is now the new universal language. We navigate our world with images, from traffic signs to toilet doors. The image has revolutionized revolutions (in the form of Che Guevara T-shirts) and brought down barriers. From televised images of the Vietnam War to VCR tapes of American films entering Russia, from cassettes of the Ayatollah's return to Iran to images of the fall of the Berlin Wall and China's famed Great Firewall — images have changed the face of the modern world in just a few decades. As Leonard Shlain says, 'No culture can successfully shut out pictorial information for long anymore. The Iconic Revolution, surfing along on electromagnetic waves, will ultimately crest any man-made obstacle. When a culture shifts its emphasis from written words to iconic information, it will experience tumult. The reverse is also true.'[7] In the beginning was not the word, but the image; as seen on cave walls the world over. Now the tables are turning and the image, and the ethereal, is making a comeback.

The neon tribes adorn themselves with today's iconographic markings. It is now fashionable to decorate the body with images. The latest trends are in colorful and elaborate tattoos. The new neon tribes are image conscious and creatively proselytizing the body as a communication carrier. The physical body is hybridizing with the iconic digital worlds, marking our partnerships. The emerging global, twenty-first century hieroglyphics are recombining the logographic and alphabetic elements to stream a revised and updated reality simulacrum into being. Our real-time data streaming is creating what David Gelernter once referred to as *Mirror Worlds*, similar to a simulation of our real world. In the image of our world we are replicating the magical traditions of Hermeticism and Kabbalah, forging a reflective Gnostic representation of the origin so that we may gaze back upon the unknowable designer (or coder). The Renaissance magus has morphed and splintered into a profusion of youthful coders, hackers, and preteen programmers. The Hermetist of yore is now robed in the anonymous, masked hacker navigating not the medieval labyrinth but the new media mindscape.

NEW MEDIA, NEW MIND

Societies have always been shaped more by the nature of the media by which men communicate than by the content of the communication.
— Marshall McLuhan, *From Cliché to Archetype*

McLuhan was right to spot that technologies become extensions of ourselves. In his early days many people thought McLuhan's ideas fringe, or controversial at best. And yet McLuhan's foresight told him that there is really no separation between a person and the technology they use to navigate their reality. Every technological revolution is also a revolution in perspective. The Scientific Revolution gave us the telescope and the microscope so the 'as above, so below' could be scrutinized and mapped by the quantifying eye. The world 'out there' suddenly jumped in to reveal itself through the human cornea. Our technologies influence and reshape our language; the two are not separate entities. In turn, technology and language shape our perceptions of reality. All together they form one complete, holistic apparatus of consciousness.

McLuhan noted that after the print culture we entered the electronic era, which today has developed into the digital age. William Irwin Thompson equates this stage with the era of 'Planetization' (1945 to present), and the philosopher and linguist Jean
Gebser noted the same era as one of integral consciousness. And so we have a new triad forming that denotes this era — digital (technology), planetization (social), and integral (consciousness). Our physical reality is now becoming more complex, compressed, and interconnected, infused by the digital, the planetary, and the integral. As McLuhan said decades before:

> Today, after more than a century of electric technology, we have extended our central nervous system itself in a global embrace. . . . Rapidly, we approach the final phase of the extensions of man — the technological simulation of consciousness.[8]

Our technologies of communication and communion have now spread globally to merge us individually with humankind, and humankind with us as individuals. We all now participate in the consequences of our every action. As Aurobindo said, 'The individual has to live in humanity as well as humanity in the individual.'[9]

The technological has now caught up with us so that, in the words of McLuhan, it's a simulation of consciousness as well as an extension of our biological nervous system. We have arrived at a new nexus of transformation where 'the thing that is made of language and of image and imagination, that has resided in the monkey for so long, is now superseding biological evolution and, through culture, taking over the reins of its own form and destiny.'[10] A destiny is being reshaped in a way where the sacred energies are coming through in new forms and expressions. As a species we are communicating, and *communing,* as never before. Our outreach now provides us with the medium for a global embrace.

The World Soul — the *animus mundi* — which I discuss later in chapter thirteen, has a new medium for her presence. The external nervous system of our communication technologies (to paraphrase McLuhan) is like a blueprint for our inner technologies of the soul. McLuhan's analogy is apt, for it visualizes the inner body of humankind being turned inside out and laid across the world. In a sense this is exactly what is occurring. The inner essence of the individual is being relayed through our wireless connections. Our outer spaces are carrier waves for our inner language, for our empathy, compassion, and longing for connection.

The Internet was once feted as the 'global brain' because it was networking our billion-plus pieces of information.* And yet now the Internet, or rather the medium of our global connectivity, is networking more than information. It is sharing empathic understanding, touches of kindness, and glances of consideration—all qualities of the heart. It has become more than an extended mind, it has become the external medium for our collective species' soul. Through this new fabric that weaves human beings together across our planet we are remodeling our forms of community, imagination, and relationships.

A conscious superorganism is being birthed across the planet as billions of individual hearts and minds are sharing bits and pieces of their lives and experiences. It is a new language code, a new *communion*, creating a topography that combines technology, planet, and consciousness. It is a sacred web of human becoming. A new destiny is dawning that enfolds everybody. According to Terence McKenna:

> Our destiny is not ours to decide. It is in the hands of a weirdly democratic, amoeboid, hyperintelligent superorganism that is called Everybody. As we come to terms with this, as we take our place embedded in the body of Everybody, information flows more freely and the reality of this informational creature is seen more clearly. The fact is that we are in a symbiotic relationship with an organism made of information.[11]

---

*   For example, one of the first books to discuss this was Peter Russell's *The Awakening Earth: The Global Brain* (1984).

This flow and flux of information is only one part of the language codes that the sacred uses for its expression. The sacred has always been with us, attempting to communicate through us, only now we have co-created a more communal space for its presence. Our technologies function as magic, and magic is a technology; there is no demarcation between these mysteries. Our 'technologies of communication are always, at least potentially, technologies of the sacred, simply because the ideas and experiences of the sacred have always informed human communication.'[12] A different landscape is now emerging upon the old, and many people are still unable to see this wondrous unfolding. The technologies of soul and our soulful technologies are now constructing a new reality matrix for us to embark upon our planetary future. The sacred presence pushes up against the old world and births its revival, infusing once again our own hearts and soul. And as I discuss in the next chapter, magic never died. . . .

Notes

[1] Walter Ong, *Orality and Literacy: The Technologizing of the Word* (London: Routledge, 1982), 78.

[2] Quoted in Leonard Shlain, *The Alphabet Versus The Goddess: The Conflict Between Word and Image* (New York: Penguin, 1998), 2

[3] McKenna, *The Archaic Revival*, 64.

[4] McKenna, *The Archaic Revival*, 69.

[5] Shlain, *The Alphabet Versus The Goddess*, 417.

[6] James Burke and Robert Ornstein, *The Axemaker's Gift: A Double-Edged History of Human Culture* (New York: Putnam, 1995).

[7] Shlain, *The Alphabet Versus The Goddess*, 425.

[8] Marshall McLuhan, *Understanding Media* (London: Routledge, 2002/1964), 3.

[9] Sri Aurobindo, *The Human Cycle: The Psychology of Social Development* (Twin Lakes, WI: Lotus Light Publications, 1999/1950), 69.

[10] McKenna, *The Archaic Revival*, 32. [11] McKenna, *The Archaic Revival*, 64.

[12] Davis, *Techgnosis*, 8.

9

A SENSE OF THE SACRED: MAGIC NEVER DIED

Ancient traditions are reviving, different religions and cultures are awakening to new ways of being. . . .
— Václev Havel, address delivered at Harvard University, June 8, 1995

God is alive, magic is afoot God is alive, magic is afoot God is afoot, magic is alive Alive is afoot, magic never died
— Leonard Cohen, *Beautiful Losers*

The sense of the sacred does not require any image of god. The essence of human spirituality has flourished within humankind since before the arrival in history of religions and belief systems. What are important are not our images of what such gods may be, but rather the state of our consciousness, the beauty of our human condition, and the rightness of our human behavior. What *is* sacred is that which blesses and fulfils the dignity of all life. In other words, that which allows the sacred energy to dwell through us in our physical and interior lives upon this glorious planet.

THE SACRED REVIVAL

We have arrived at an important stage upon the human journey, and now this moment calls out for a degree of recognition. There will be no more gothic cathedrals built to exalt humankind to the heavens, no more prophets to lead humankind to the divine, and no more Holy Grails to entice humankind upon the quest. We now have the sacred suffusing us en masse, manifesting as both the tangible and intangible. Civilization is being finely renewed from the inside out by a subtle vibration that has come to us like an emanation of sunlight. Look at the conversations we are having today with each other; look at how many creative projects around the world are being instigated and led by young people. Generations before us were not discussing transcendence or the technologies of the soul. Our era has brought the inner world out into the world and into focus.

The sacred is not a concept but an experiential understanding of life beyond our limited selves — of transcendence and immersion simultaneously within and without. Only two or three generations before us there was no inner world to explore publicly. Before the rise of the psychological sciences there was no cultural language to explore the subconscious. The inner landscape of human beings was quietly explored and navigated by the mystics, seers, adepts, and initiates, who kept their traditions away from the masses, and away from persecution.

For millennia the sacred arts were defiled, harassed, and discriminated against. The magical arts also fell into this tarnished category. And yet magic and alchemy are found worldwide, in all traditional cultures, in remarkably similar manifestations, in 'a uniformity which can ultimately only result from the single unifying aim of those cultures: spiritual realization.'[1] Spiritual realization has never been a mass pursuit, but rather something pursued by individuals often classed as outsiders. And so the presence of the sacred in our societies has always been unperceived, operating unseen and under the radar. It has always been present and operating, only not in ways suspected by humankind.

Magic too has always been present in its various guises. Magic, in its original form, is that which concentrates and radiates the mind; it is a deep penetrating force field of compassion and communion. Our reality matrix is composed of energy. Everything within it is a form of energy in various states. Those states can be modified, like the fine tuning of an instrument to create a more harmonious sound. The energy that surrounds and permeates us can be raised to a higher key, resulting in new perceptions. The wisdom traditions, the perennial philosophy, speak of how human beings, by their own spiritual ascent, are able to also animate and raise up the world around them. The emanation of the sacred, spiritual energies furthers the spiritual realization within matter reality.

Most of what is today labeled as supernatural is but the residue of the sacred inherent in humankind and the world. It is there, no matter how we ignore or discard it. It is this residue that tingles within us, and creates our sense of dissatisfaction and our indefinable taste of disconnection. Unbeknownst to us, we recreate this sense of the sacred through our pursuits and pastimes. Again, it is the *howl*, the 'burning for the ancient heavenly connection to the starry dynamo in the machinery of night.' We sometimes mock it through our pseudo attempts at spirituality, yet that which is true shall remain longer than the ability of the superficial to entice us.

Magic may shock the profane, yet it has existed as a core experience long before we had any sense of what it actually was. As historian and scholar Arthur Versluis notes:

> The reason that magic is not in good standing in the West is that it is based upon the fundamental unity of man and cosmos and so is in conflict with the inherent dualism of the modern outlook. But magic will be in existence long after the modern era has disappeared: it cannot be otherwise, for magic is the physical expression of the eternal, inner, spiritual transmutation.[2]

When it comes to the eternal, inner, spiritual transmutation, there are no absolute laws, just the continual unfolding. The world we see, our reality matrix, is a reflection of the being we are, and the state we are in. As human beings, we each interact with the world differently because we *perceive* the world differently. In interacting differently we each contribute to creating a different world. The sacred reality understands that we exist as part of a participatory cosmos. It is this sacredness without a name that infuses the human condition. To be a human being is to be inherently imbued with a spiritual force that animates us in ways we are largely unaware of. And yet through this animated force we see the world around us. It cultivates our worldview, our values, and is the source of our quest for meaning. And a civilization's worldview is its most precious possession.

Everything proceeds from this primary perception — a collective gaze of wonder, or perhaps of limitation. As philosopher E. A. Burtt noted, 'It is the ultimate picture which an age forms of the nature of its world that is its most fundamental possession.'[3] The basic, fundamental understanding is that we cannot observe the world without changing it. Our presence, and the resulting perceptions that arise, are developed within specific cultural environments. These cultural contexts construct the lens through which we view our life and our sense of reality. These constructs could be religious, secular, or anything in between.

We are a mixture of the essential with the accumulated. It is within this amalgamation of our lives that we find much of our struggle. And yet the presence of the sacred is so crucial in our lives that without it our status as humans itself is in question. The sacred order of the past existed at a time when the world was different, when its needs were different. As philosopher Henryk Skolimowski notes, 'Older spiritualties were created in response to different problems, within the context of a different worldview, and in order to articulate different dimensions of the human condition. *Spirituality is an articulated essence of the human condition of a given time.*'[4] At each moment we articulate the human condition in the context of our times. The sacred energies and the spiritual impulses are a medium and a means through which we come to learn of and express the human condition. And these expressions are in response to a shifting and unfolding understanding of the cosmos and of our reality matrix.

Before the emergence of structured religions, the human condition articulated itself in 'pre-religious' forms of spirituality. Whatever the times, the sacred impulse attempts to be known. For great periods the sacred impulse was almost invisible within human societies, as we struggled with the raw energies of brute materiality, 'red in tooth and claw' and cloaked in mechanical rationalism. Yet now, as I attempt to explain within these pages, the sacred impulse is raising its head again in new cultural forms, expressions, and mediums.

Magic has a role in helping to give shape and substance to our meanings. Magic teaches us that the way forward, the way to heal the rift in our reality matrix, is by the uniting of the spiritual and the profane, the celestial and the mundane. In our reality, each day lived is an expression of the spiritual and the sacred existing through us, invisible as a silent breath. And yet the magic never died; magic is still alive, magic is afoot (to paraphrase Leonard Cohen). For us now, 'the greatest danger to us shall arise, not because of 'magic,' but rather if true magic, true transmutation, should disappear.'[5] The world is becoming an exciting, magical, and mysterious domain once again. And as later chapters discuss, technology is likewise moving from its position as a brute, mechanistic hardware to a fluid, almost seamless, magical part of our augmented reality.

The world is reviving its sense of being a *mysterium tremendum*, a sacred place to dwell in. To live the sacred revival is about reflecting a light that comes through us, for all of us and the planet. As beacons we must pass it on, and we must also light up the way for each traveler upon the path. The truth is a spiritualizing force that actualizes through us. The sacred impulse is also the creative and dynamic force of transcendence. And yet it must be a sacred energy for *our times*. It must be alive and relevant, otherwise it becomes another relic to be idolized and venerated rather than *lived*. The sense of the sacred is of a *living work*.

Our physical global body, made up of systems and structures, is responding to this need by shifting from top-down structures to decentralized networks. As discussed in the previous chapter, our new modes of communication are meshing us in a web, a planetary embrace that is organically creating, cell by cell, a new species body. As this unfolds we need to meet this transformation by changing the ways we think, by altering the ways we *do* things, and by allowing consciousness and the sacred energies to flow into the world, to flow *through us.* That is, to manifest the qualities, attitudes, and our presence in the world that will most effectively receive, hold, and transmit this consciousness. This responsibility is also a part of our living work right now.

The days of working in seclusion are over — the new sacred energy does not support monasticism. The sacred must connect fluidly between our inner and outer worlds; it is not a monastic endeavor but exists within the active folds, avenues, and marketplaces of life. High castles, priestly enclaves, guru sanctuaries, etc., are edifices of the past where a different energy was contained. The sacred revival of today is a nurturing, feminine energy that comes alive *through people*. The sacred revival stands as comfortable with the spandex superhero mutants on our screens as it does with the appreciative touch, the supportive word, the reassuring glance that we each can weave into our lives. This is the sacred impulse for our times — that which is a part of the living substance that comes through us. It is a *living soul* that holds within it the species body. As Meister Eckhart said, 'The soul is not in the body; the body is in the soul.'

The sacred revival is already affecting us, infecting our thinking patterns and consciousness, whether we are aware of it or not. Our perspectives on the world and the cosmos have been changing dramatically over recent years. Most of those who consider the issue of life in the cosmos have come to a realization that we do not exist as part of a dead universe. Even our sciences, our telescopes, are pointing their attention toward intelligent life in the cosmos. We are closing in, slowly metamorphosing out of our cocoon of cosmic quarantine. Human beings are also forced to transcend beyond the conditioned cocoon we sleep within. As Skolimowski says, 'A unique feature of our humanness in us is not only the courage to be but *the courage to become*, the courage to continually transcend every station we have reached.'[6] A part of our transformation—of our *becoming*—is the recognition that the human being is a sacred particle in a sacred universe.

Enchantment has been humanity's natural state for eons. The innate state of humanity is to feel integral to all life. This provided for the integrity of the human psyche. This continuity has only been disrupted for a number of centuries, whereas our state of enchantment has been with us for millennia. It is time we return to that enchantment and reconnection with a source of meaning. Those streams of significance, those waters of wisdom, have always been with us. It only depended upon whether we wished to get our feet wet or not. As Terence McKenna put it:

> Imagine if every problem were solved appropriately, if every relationship evolved appropriately, if every act were an appropriate one. That alone would be the kingdom of heaven. And that is, I think, what we're pushing toward. Not cosmic fireworks or the descent

> of alien beings in flying saucers, but simply appropriate activity — empowered, felt experience — and the abandonment of the illusion of separateness.[7]

This indeed is what is pushing through the fabric of our societies, as the old energies cling to their fear and divisive strategies. As Rilke wrote, 'We are the bees of the invisible,' and our task as individuals is for each of us to be a channel for the transmutation of the familiar things of this world into the transcendent.

The sacred impulse works through the planet, the living species, and also each individual. As we come together, increasingly so through the medium of our technologies, we each can bring a spark into the burning flame of the living work of our transmutation. As Sri Aurobindo understood, our sacred revival (what he considered as a spiritual age) must 'be preceded by the appearance of an increasing number of individuals who are no longer satisfied with the normal intellectual, vital and physical existence of man, but perceive that a greater evolution is the real goal of humanity and attempt to effect it in themselves, to lead others to it and to make it the recognized goal of the race.'[8] The antithesis of the sacred revival, those who attempt the reverse of leading others toward transition, seek their power in the sorcery of psychological control and manipulation, also now on a mass scale. Yet the call, the sacred impulse, beats within each one of us. For some, admittedly, it is louder than others.

The sacred presence is a reflection of the individual soul as well as the world soul. It is a technology of the soul to know and operate from the true self, the essential self, otherwise we are not whole. The integral communion of the soul is between the inner world of the individual (the individual soul), and the physical world outside of us. It is a synthesis which gives us meaning. If we do not renew our task daily by reflecting upon the soul, we do an injustice to ourselves. And yet this is no easy task. As Sogyal Rinpoche says:

> Looking in will require of us great subtlety and great courage — nothing less than a complete shift in our attitude to life and to the mind. We are so addicted to looking outside ourselves that we have lost access to our inner being almost completely. We are terrified to look inward, because our culture has given us no idea of what we will find.[9]

No other relationship can be achieved that is higher than the one you have with the sacred essence within yourself. Life must have meaning for us before we can bring authentic meaning into the lives of others. Maybe Pierre Teilhard de Chardin said it best when he said that sacred human 'becoming' is not only 'open to a few of the privileged nor to one chosen people to the exclusion of all others' but rather is 'in a direction in which *all together* can join and find completion in a spiritual regeneration of the earth.'[10]

Our ancestors were aware that they lived in a sacred cosmos where the physical world existed in communion with the unseen dimension which ensouled and sanctified it. There was no rigid line drawn between what was the inner world and what was external reality, because both domains were in correspondence. The individual human soul was a part of the greater sacred reality. And just as the sacred is an instrument of the human, so the human is an instrument of the sacred. The sacred worldview is one that accepts not only the metaphysical but also the magical and the mysterious, the magnificent wonder in everything and all. And as we evolve, individually and as a species, so too will we become intelligible to ourselves, and become capable of recognizing the true nature of reality. Until we reach that state, all truths are relative. Christopher Bache, through his own journeys into transpersonal psychology, came to understand that the entire universe is 'a unified organism of extraordinary design reflecting a massive Creative Intelligence.'[11] We are each of us a piece of that sacred, creative intelligence. As written on a 2,500-year-old Orphic tablet: 'I am a child of earth and starry heaven, but my race is of heaven alone.'

As part of that quest, we must bathe in the moon's rivers that are now arising. . . .

Notes

[1] Arthur Versluis, *The Philosophy of Magic* (London: Arkana, 1986), 2.

[2] Versluis, *The Philosophy of Magic*, 129.

[3] Cited in David Fideler, *Restoring the Soul of the World: Our Living Bond with Nature's Intelligence* (Rochester, Vermont: Inner Traditions, 2014), 181.

[4] Henryk Skolimowski, *A Sacred Place to Dwell: Living With Reverence Upon the Earth* (Shaftesbury, Dorset: Element, 1993), 1.

[5] Versluis, *The Philosophy of Magic*, 125.

[6] Skolimowski, *A Sacred Place to Dwell*, 100.

[7] McKenna, *The Archaic Revival*, 22-3.

[8] Aurobindo, *The Human Cycle*, 263.

[9] Hollis, *Tracking the Gods*, 148.

[10] Quoted in Davis, *Techgnosis*, 317.

[11] Quoted in Anne Baring, *The Dream of the Cosmos: A Quest for the Soul* (Dorset: Archive Publishing, 2013), 332.

10

MOON RIVER:
A NEW SACRED MARRIAGE
OF THE MASCULINE AND FEMININE

O Awaken not the Beauty until the time comes.
— Inscription in Chartres Cathedral

When the moon shall shine as bright as the sun, the Messiah will come.
— Baal Shem Tov

Let us be honest on the matter — as a dominant species on this planet, we haven't been very nice to the feminine of late. And by the word 'feminine' I don't just mean women or the body of women, but the *whole body* of feminine soul. This is what connects us to all things, and through which everything flows. As Anne Baring puts it:

> The word 'Feminine' stands for the Soul and the unseen cosmic web of life that connects each one of us to all others and to the life of the planet and the greater life of the Cosmos. It stands for the recognition that we live within a Sacred Order and that we have a responsibility to protect the life of the planet and all the variety of species it embraces instead of exploiting them

> for the benefit of our species alone. In sum, the word 'Feminine' stands for a totally different perspective on life, a totally different worldview or paradigm of reality and for the feeling values which might reflect and support that worldview. It stands for a new planetary consciousness and the arduous creation of a new kind of civilization.[1]

The word 'feminine' can also be understood as an aspect of consciousness that imbibes the cosmos. Everything that is not a part of this feminine soul has a tangible relation to separation and separateness. In Western civilization especially the quest for freedom, the desire to explore and conquer new territories, to strive for ideologies of scientific and technological progress, has largely been dominated by a masculine energy. It is the energy that seeks end goals; it requires results and accomplishments. It desires to go beyond limitations, for better or for worse, where the ends often justify the means. This masculine urge has pushed forward as a deep impulse, not only for discovery but for legacy. The masculine impulse wants to secure a lasting physical legacy, while the feminine influence seeks a gentle eternity in the evermore.

In the relative recent history of our species on this planet, that is, for the previous two millennia at least, we have strayed away from the feminine influence, both in spirit and in image. That is why the sacred revival insists on a new sanctified marriage of the masculine and feminine aspects of the evermore. It is not really an option, it is a necessity. The effects on our planet from the neglect of the feminine have been dramatic. In many ways it is similar to the loss of soul connection. It is a lessening of the instinctive knowledge over acquired knowledge. It is a loss of the reverence for the interconnection and sanctity of life, a dwindling of our trust in the power of the imagination, and a shrinking away from our compassionate participation with a playful and creative cosmos. The feminine and the masculine are forms of being that correspond to how we process consciousness. Often when speaking of these terms I am referring to modes of consciousness that have shaped our perspectives and worldviews, and hence our social and cultural environments. I am not speaking of gender, sexuality, or of physical bodies. I refer to the energy of being that we choose to respond and act from.

    The masculine consciousness is also behind the image of a divinity that belongs to the heavens. From 'up there,' the dominance of a masculine god has made it permissible to develop a science that would 'torture Nature's secrets from her' and thus take control over our environment.* The materially driven modern cultures that arose from this mode of domination resonate with the alienation and individualism reflected by the remoteness of a masculine god. The notion of a restored perfection, for the new Adam, was a male ideal that successive generations of monks, magi, and Masons have

---

*   A reference to Sir Francis Bacon, whose scientific method became the foundations for modern empirical science.

all striven for under the almost religious pursuit of technology. Through this path, modern life divorced itself from the sacred, integral interdependence of the wholeness of creative life.

As mystic scholar Llewellyn Vaughan-Lee says, 'Men have a deep fear of woman's magical nature and over the centuries many patterns of repression have been imposed to deny her access to her magical power.'[2] This comment reflects back upon the witch hunts from the sixteenth to the eighteenth century in Europe, where tens of thousands of women accused of being witches were put to death. The executioners were almost exclusively men who represented the church hierarchy. This was a masculine energy that for millennia had been parading and swinging its heavy paternal axe of hierarchical power. And the witches were yet another manifestation of female power that the ecclesiastical authorities could not tolerate.

Some of these so-called witches were women who knew about herbs, how to heal and nurture people, or simply how to listen to nature, while the majority were purely the innocent victims of malicious gossip or misplaced fear. One of the many things they were accused of was gathering and conspiring together. How did they gather? They gathered in witches' *circles*. Here we have the energy of hierarchical power against the energy of circular, relational flow. It was also the fear of a magical presence within the feminine that fueled a deep repression, which over the centuries has become a pattern—the denial of the subtle, the integral, the nurturing. According to certain documents, over 80 percent of accused witches were female. In other words, witch hunting was by and large 'women hunting.' As a chronicler in 1600 wrote, 'Demons take no account of males . . . and among a hundred witches, there's scarcely a man to be seen.'[3]

The masculine consciousness likes to be visible and make its imprint known, whereas feminine energy is subtler. The downside to this has been that our societies have predominantly valued that which is visible, and reject or ignore that which is less tangible. On top of this, it has been suggested that the rise of literacy also contributed to the repression of the feminine. According to Leonard Shlain:

> Due to its exceedingly short learning curve, every society that has acquired alphabet literacy has become violently self-destructive a short time afterward. This madness has been associated with a virulent misogyny and spelled trouble for images, women's rights, goddesses, and right-brain values.[4]

I am not searching to lay blame here, whether it be on literacy or church power hierarchies, as all that we experience are manifestations of consciousness that frame how we view the world. In each epoch, in each developmental phase of human evolution, we process a different mode of consciousness. As I explain further in the next chapter, these modes are often divided into 'consensus' (good), or 'heretic' (bad), and have contributed to the stunted perceptions of our reality matrix. Yet these categories of mind are aspects of grander epochs of consciousness. What we have experienced in our recent history has been the shift from a lunar to a solar epochal consciousness.

THE SHIFT FROM LUNAR TO SOLAR

Our earlier ancestors lived within a different sense of the reality matrix. Many of our premodern cultures were animated by a sense of living within a sacred order, and were shamanic by aspects if not by practice. These premodern, shamanic cultures had an instinct for relationship and connection. They exhibited a type of consciousness that anthropologist Lucien Lévy-Bruhl described as *participation mystique*. Cultural historian Richard Tarnas notes:

> This participation mystique involves a complex sense of direct inner participation not only of human beings in the world but also of human beings in the divine powers, through ritual, and of divine powers in the world, by virtue of their immanent and transformative presence.[5]

This sense of the transformative presence, the *participation mystique*, framed the consciousness that defined the 'Lunar Era.' The Lunar Era shared a mythology across its cultures that included some, or all, of the following themes: death and rebirth, descent and return from the underworld, struggle with a superhuman adversary, journey or quest, transformation, sacred marriage, and birth of a divine child or soul.[6]

In the Lunar Era, the feminine principle was predominant and represented the matrix, or web, of hidden relationships through which spirit and nature — the visible and invisible dimensions of life and the cosmos — were connected with each other. This feminine energy manifested as a cosmic dimension of soul, as an inherent sacred order that bound all visible and nonvisible realms. The consciousness of this era recognized the sacredness of life and the presence of the goddess, according to Ann Baring:

> She announces herself to be the source, ground or matrix of all forms of life; the fertile womb which eternally regenerates plants, animals, human beings; the life-force which attracts the male to the female; the power which creates, destroys, and regenerates all forms of itself. She speaks as the source and embodiment of all instinctive processes. She is the life-force which is nurturing, compassionate, beneficent, but also the terrifying and implacable force of destruction which can manifest as volcanic eruption, earthquake, flood, drought and disease.[7]

The divine feminine lies at the heart of many Western quest mythologies, such as Odysseus returning home to Penelope under the guidance of Athena, Theseus following Ariadne's thread through the Cretan labyrinth, Dante's journey through the underworld to find his Beatrice, and the medieval quest for the Holy Grail. All these quests frame the need to connect with the imminent and transcendent feminine principle. Yet, as in all cycles, the Lunar Era passed and in its place came what has been called the Solar Era.

The shift from a lunar to a solar consciousness, around 2000 BCE, triggered a new phase in the development of Western civilization. Most significant was the break from the participation mystique of the Lunar Era. Historians have pointed to two principal factors that contributed in the shift from lunar to solar cultures. The first of these was physical, and had to do with the energy of conquest and control as a wave of invasions swept over the lands. The agricultural communities of the Fertile Crescent saw great change come upon them in around 2200 BCE. The reasons for this could be numerous, such as a change in climate that resulted in forcing communities to seek new territories. Whatever the reasons, the resulting changes saw invaders on horseback bringing with them their male sky gods. Similarly, the Sea Peoples invaded from the Mediterranean, bringing with them their conquering masculine attributes and ideals. War and conquest became the new devastating theme of the age where Egyptian, Babylonian, and Assyrian mythologies tell of warlike leaders idealized for their violent victories.

The Lunar Era imbibed the soul of the cosmos as part of the sacred order of life. Human life — its rituals and culture — participated in the grand mythic nature of the world. In contrast, the Solar Era consciousness that came in so forcibly was focused on the conquest and mastery of nature, and celebrated those potent individuals whose power separated them out from the tribal group community. The solar hero is the warrior, with attributes of a masculine deity (later the god of the three Abrahamic religions). This sky god was the creator of the heavens and the earth, and everything that lay in between. And yet the deity itself lay separate from its creation, distant and beyond. In this was born the division between creator and creation; between nature and spirit. This shift to the Solar Era consciousness initiated a new phase in the perception of life. Humanity's worldview shifted to where it saw nature as something to be controlled and manipulated, while some far distant deity in the skies could no longer be found within nature.

The sun became the new focus of consciousness. The hero was no longer the shaman or priestess who navigates between worlds, venturing into the otherworld, but the outstanding warrior who fights in light against the darkness to vanquish his enemies. From *The Epic of Gilgamesh* to the Babylonian creation myth *Enuma Elish*, the 'battle of a hero-god and his conquest of the dragon/monster of darkness, chaos and evil became the dominant theme of all the hero myths of the solar era.'[8] The Solar Era consciousness gave rise to the concept of the holy war, the dualistic notion of the victory of good over evil, and the means of human sacrifice in war to justify the goal. It is this mythology of the Solar Era consciousness which is petering out today and yet in its final gasps of power has created the current contested mythology surrounding the War on Terror. The permanent war without a definable enemy, with the potential enemy being among us, friend as foe, is a creation from the solar consciousness. This thinking has even infiltrated into our corporate world and influences the modern male psyche. In our institutions of knowledge the need to race and win over our rivals is the warrior spirit that is often conditioned into us from an early age. Our edifices of investigation and inquiry are patented as masculine realms. As an example, Thomas Sprat, the historian of the Royal Society (the great center of learning founded in 1660 in London), dubbed its domain as the 'Masculine Arts of Knowledge.' The emergence of the powerful image of a male deity also shifted our cultural consciousness away from the earthly, nurturing womb of the Mother Goddess toward the logos of the Father.

This brings us to the second principal factor which has been credited as contributing to the shift from lunar to solar cultures—the rise of literacy. The written word eventually came to replace the oral traditions of the lunar cultures. Literacy, it has been noted, preferentially reinforces the left brain's dominance over the right hemisphere. As we now know from recent neurological studies, the left hemisphere dominates in areas of language, logic, causality, and linear processing. It is the part of the mind that focuses on achieving end goals in spite of the means. Perhaps, as Leonard Shlain points out: 'Only because we have recently shifted to an alternative method of processing information have we been able to gain a perspective on the alphabet's role in the repression of women.'[9] This is a controversial hypothesis and the jury is still out on this one. However, it is interesting, as Shlain notes, that 'the religious wars that wracked Europe in the 150 years after the printing press had transformed European culture can be viewed as a sort of mass madness. They occurred only in those lands impacted by the printing press; the steeper the rise of literacy rates the more ferocious the religious wars were.'[10] What is clear is that the consciousness that dominated the Solar Era exhibited dominant masculine attributes.

The Solar Era developed and celebrated the strong individual, and with this came the rise of the conscious ego which also laid the groundwork for the later rational mind. Yet the price to be paid has been high, as the sacred impulse was driven out of the world and back into shadow. The reality matrix of the Solar Era saw no place for the nurturing instinct or for the role of intuition. Creative imagination became an outsider, the affectation of daydreamers. In the Solar Era phase of our evolution the human psyche was split between the conscious rational mind (the hero) and the older power of instinct (the dragon). And, like good old Saint George, we've been fighting dragons ever since!

The consciousness of the modern human, the consciousness of modernity (as discussed earlier), has cut itself off from the sacred, from the source of the magical realm, from the imaginal otherworld that infuses our reality matrix. It has almost succeeded in disassociating itself entirely from this source, but not totally. The sacred revival is once again seeking presence, acknowledgment, and expression within our cultural consciousness. It wishes for us to live *within it*, and to fully participate in this nurtured embrace. And so we might ask ourselves whether the journey from the Lunar Era through the Solar Era was a necessary stage in our evolutionary transcendence.

The energetic force behind the solar, masculine impulse must surely now have to come to terms with the feminine principle. The sacred calls out for a recovery of wholeness as the new integral consciousness seeps into our reality matrix. The sacred remarriage of the older lunar consciousness with the incumbent solar consciousness will serve to provide us with a grander and more inclusive perception of reality.

THE SACRED MARRIAGE

The Hasidic saint Baal Shem Tov said, as quoted at the head of this chapter, 'When the moon shall shine as bright as the sun, the Messiah will come.' This can be seen as representing the lunar consciousness (moon) shining as bright as the solar consciousness (sun) resulting in the Messiah (a balanced integral, holistic consciousness). This harmonious outcome, this messianic savior, is a conscious, sacred, cosmic worldview that honors the feminine principle. This is the alchemical marriage between sun and moon. The alchemists had the notion of *unus mundus,* a unifying cosmic ground in which both matter and psyche (soul) participate. This is the union between the masculine and feminine energies, which together form the unified *unus mundus.* This sacred marriage of the lunar and solar consciousness, in mythological terms, results in the birth of the 'child,' which represents a new integral consciousness arising within the collective human species that recognizes the sacredness of the reality matrix.

This sacred consciousness revival has its own modern mythology in our recent communion with Earth's lunar satellite, the moon. The Apollo program succeeded in making six spaceflights and placing twelve human beings on the moon. From these spaceflights we have received spectacular vistas and visions of the Earth from afar. The most popular of these photos, 'Earthrise,' showed the Earth rising from beyond the moon's surface, and was taken by astronaut William Anders in 1968 during the Apollo 8 mission. This photograph has been credited with catalyzing a change in the human mind, and even with triggering the environmental movement. It was the first time our species had gained a vision of the beautiful homeland from off-planet. Its effect was startling, and not only on those who remained on the ground, gazing up. Several astronauts have confessed their epiphanies of experiencing the spectacle of outer space. Edgar Mitchell, astronaut on the Apollo 14 mission and sixth person to walk on the moon, had this response:

> My mind was flooded with an intuitive knowing that everything is interconnected—that this magnificent universe is a harmonious, directed, purposeful whole. And that we humans, both as individuals and as a species, are an integral part of the ongoing process of creation.[11]

Gene Cernan, the last astronaut to leave the moon (on Apollo 17), had a similar epiphany: 'I stood in the blue darkness and looked in awe at the earth from the lunar surface. What I saw was too beautiful to grasp—there was too much logic, too much purpose. It was too beautiful to have happened by accident.'[12]

In leaving Earth we explored the moon, the age-old symbol of the Great Mother, the feminine, and the soul. By leaving Gaia's earthly folds, from having the vision of earthrise from space, humanity was lifted beyond its petty earthbound nationalisms. Humanity experienced an expansion in perception and consciousness—a small step toward a fully extended mind. It was also a trigger moment in the sacred rebirth of the feminine impulse back into the collective soul of our species. A sacred energy began to reawaken out of its darkness and back into the light, reaching for the intuitive and the visible within a multitude of longing hearts. It marked the time to reconnect to the soulful guidance and wisdom of the feminine impulse. The revival of the sacred feminine has an important part to play in the emerging planetary consciousness. Our human compassion and intelligence can now begin to find conscious expression and participate in both planetary and cosmic life. In the words of Jungian psychologist Anne Baring:

> This powerful evolutionary impulse, reconnecting us to our deepest instincts for relationship with each other and with the life of the planet, is working a profound alchemy beneath the surface of our culture. Women and men are participating in a process of transformation that is manifesting as a new planetary consciousness, a new cultural impulse whose emphasis is on the growing recognition of the interconnection and interdependence of all aspects of life.[13]

This growing recognition of the interconnection and interdependence that Baring speaks of is also emerging through the new global web that binds us.

The feminine impulse has already entered into our global systems, infrastructure, and technologies. It has been the energy behind the restructuring and recalibrations now unsettling our societies. This has been born out in the shifts now taking place as many top-down hierarchical systems are transitioning to bottom-up, decentered and distributed systems. The most prominent example of this is in our global technologies of communication. As I discussed in a previous book, the mode of communication has shifted from one-to-one (for example, television), to many-to-many (digital communications, such as the Internet).* Our vastly expanding digital world is more than a communication device, more than an 'Inter-net,' and more than a world of information and other goodies — it is now a symbiotic part of life on this planet.

Humanity has always been a part of symbiotic life on this planet. Nothing, no species, exists in isolation. Symbiotic humanity is now extending this relationship into a technological partnership. It is a partnership of *technoosis*, as the *tech*nosphere and the *noo*sphere create another sacred marriage.** It is another alchemical bonding as matter and mind merge and coalesce further into a unified field of immersion, cohesion, and communication. And now this transformation is being played out in our global societies, gradually and in diverse rhythms. As scientist and futurist Joël de Rosnay notes, the 'transition to symbiotic society calls for biological and ecological concepts, those involving communications, transversality, and networks, and this reveals the need for new, feminine values.'[14]

These feminine values are inherent in how our increasingly complex and decentralized networks are

---

* See The Phoenix Generation: A New Era of Connection, Compassion and Consciousness (2014).

** An invented amalgam of technosphere and noosphere not to be confused with Erik Davis's Techgnosis.

recalibrating the ways we connect and communicate. New initiatives, innovations, projects, friendships, and relations are emerging from our interconnected *technoosis*. The new multiplicities are undermining the once dominant masculine consciousness and energy. The new collaborative spaces are all about multitasking, from share economies to information swapping. The global platform has increasingly become a place for such issues as human rights, education, health care, child care, welfare, and the environment. These mounting issues, as well as the manner of how they are multitasked and openly discussed, all belong to the gatherer/nurturer instinct rather than the hunter/killer. In other words, the nurturing and meaning of relationships traditionally belong to the feminine, and in the past our technological developments were not always resonant with the feminine energy. Yet now our emerging digital technologies are creating, forming, and opening up new pathways and interconnections for the feminine impulse to enter and permeate our material world. Our physical institutions and systems are responding to this new intervention by shifting from top-down structures to distributed and decentralized networks. The feminine energy/consciousness now has a crucial role to play in the development of our new technologies and the emerging *technoosis*, which is all a part of the sacred revival. Yet before great and lasting change can occur within our human civilization we first need to shed the monkey mind.

Notes

[1] Baring, *The Dream of the Cosmos*, 221.

[2] Llewellyn Vaughan-Lee, *The Return of the Feminine and the World Soul* (Point Reyes, CA: The Golden Sufi Center, 2009), 83.

[3] Quoted in Shlain, *The Alphabet Versus The Goddess*, 364.

[4] Shlain, *The Alphabet Versus The Goddess*, 377.

[5] Richard Tarnas, *Cosmos and Psyche: Intimations of a New World View* (London: Plume, 2007), 16.

[6] Baring, *The Dream of the Cosmos*, 73.

[7] Baring, *The Dream of the Cosmos*, 72.

[8] Baring, *The Dream of the Cosmos*, 113.

[9] Shlain, *The Alphabet Versus The Goddess*, 429.

[10] Shlain, *The Alphabet Versus The Goddess*, 361.

[11] Quoted in Baring, *The Dream of the Cosmos*, 228.

[12] Quoted in Baring, *The Dream of the Cosmos*, 227.

[13] Baring, *The Dream of the Cosmos*, 238.

[14] Joel de Rosnay, *The Symbiotic Man: A New Understanding of the Organization of Life and a Vision of the Future* (New York: McGraw Hill, 2000), 236.

11

THE NEW HERETICS:
SHEDDING THE MONKEY MIND

Every society has a cognitive structure of permissible knowledge that is managed by an elite and forbidden knowledge that is distributed in black or shadow markets by cognitive outlaws, heretics, revolutionaries, or just plain crazies.
— William Irwin Thompson, Coming Into Being

No such thing as a profane domain really exists, but only a profane point of view.
— Rene Guenon, The Reign of Quantity and the Signs of the Times

No mind, no world.
— Anaxagoras

Human consciousness changes with time, and thus likewise so do our truths. As the human mind articulates more knowledge, so does the cosmos become more intelligent to us, and also *for us*. Our human concepts of truth are always partial, always fragmentary and incomplete, for they are reflections of our own imperfections and incompleteness. And yet human consciousness is our medium, our *technology*, through which we appreciate our reality and through which reality is able to appreciate itself. In human civilization our cultures serve as the foundries that forge the truth for us, specific for each epoch.

Every culture creates its cosmology, its coherent world picture, and thus invariably creates boundaries for this cosmology. Those thinking patterns or ideas that do not fit in with the artificially constructed coherency are labeled as heretical. These are non-natural distinctions—the boundaries, parameters, and perimeters—erected by the human mind. The mind makes the world. Each culture considers its worldview superior. Just as each culture teaches its own history based on biased history texts, so does each society layer the mind with biased thinking. In other words: 'We are happy victims of our culture's perspectives because we acquired them with our mother's milk.'[1] The modern worldview has taken it upon itself to believe that its view *is* the world, rather than a particular view *of* the world. The distinction may appear slight, yet its consequences are far-reaching.

Our own transformations, our transcendence beyond our conditioning, will always be opposed by the assumptions inherent in our social systems. To wish to break from ingrained patterns and conditioned viewpoints will always get labeled as heretical. A heretic of the conscious mind is not a bad heretic to be. The evolution of human civilization has always been dependent upon such heretics. We can choose what type of myth we use to frame our view of life and the world, yet we do not have the choice of using no myth frame at all. The world we see through our senses is our map of the world, while the human mind, through a projected consciousness, unfolds the world to us. Yet this can be a trap for us as much as liberation. We can become trapped inside the matrix of our mind's models if we are not open to flexibility and variation. Culture has a way of not being open to such flexibility, and innovative ideas and minds often experience intimidation at the outset, shunned by a world preferring to cling to its shores of safety against the tides of visionary heretics. Such cultural conservatism 'can be seen as a philosophy of small minds which are happy to serve the status quo and confine themselves to established niches, forgetting that the imperative of life is to unfold, to change, to transcend.'[2]

Ludwig Fleck, a Polish microbiologist, noticed an unusual phenomenon with his students. When his new, untrained students were given microscopic sections to observe, initially they were unable to make out the observations. They could not see what was there because they had no training in *how* to look using a microscope. This showed to Ludwig Fleck (and to the rest of us) that perception requires training, and it is first necessary to learn how to see the patterns. Many of our culturally biased perceptions are sharpened and focused to see reality in a selective way. When we enlarge our capacity for conscious reflection, we enlarge our participation with the cosmos.

Our capacity of mind is a window of perception. We either view through a small aperture or a larger one, like looking out from a room with a view. Our universal laws are based on abstract reason, whether through the dogma of reason (science), or the dogma of unreason (religion). The current cult of scientific reason has led us to believe that physics and mathematics is the only way to read the universe. In other words, that participation with the cosmos or any cosmic intelligence is through the power of equations. The world, the universe, our sense of meaning, may be little else to us than a set of perspectives that are constantly shifting. What makes us think that our way of *seeing* the world today is the right one? Or any better than alternative perspectives? Each of us bets our life on some picture of reality. We should therefore ask ourselves of this picture: Does it feel deeply, intuitively right? And does it continue to feel right as times goes on?

Our modern worldview, which forms our reality matrix, is a realm of abstractions that we have constructed into sound bites and vision blocks. It appears coherent to us, yet on the contrary is fragmented, artificial, and lacking in communal presence. It also lacks our deep understanding and appreciation. The modern perception, largely belonging to the Western mind, is one that is lacking in the understanding of correspondence. We have been positioned into a dualism of objective vs. subjective, where it has to be one or the other, yet cannot be a correspondence or participation involving both. In truth, neither absolutes exist. They are the inventions of human thought models and as such are representative of our state of thinking rather than anything else. Such thinking patterns tell us that nothing is sacred. We live in secular fluidity which accepts multiple truths amid the fragmentation. If reality is a jigsaw, then our overactive rational minds have just deliberately jumbled the pieces of this jigsaw.

Each system of knowledge that we embrace is according to time and place, and so is only a specific form of articulation concerning our reality matrix. No one form, or specific articulation, is absolute. From our articulations we form our perceptions of reality. As philosopher Henryk Skolimowski says:

> The mind never conceives of bits of reality independent of each other. We always comprehend in large patterns. These patterns are known as cultures, systems of philosophy, systems of beliefs, or the architecture of the individual mind. They render reality in specific ways. This rendering, as we remember, should really be called *realitying*: transforming reality while comprehending it. We *reality* in specific patterns. These patterns are usually large. . . . *Realitying*, or *reality-making*, occurs within paradigms.[3]

These paradigms of rendered reality have formed our philosophies and cosmologies over past epochs, from the Greek mind to the Renaissance, and yet we continue to lack a cosmology that grasps the core dynamics of the creative and 'intelligent' cosmos in which we exist. Each epoch in human civilization demands a corresponding cosmology in which to frame it, and which also guides its ethos. We are at that stage of a new phase now, and have been entering into it for several decades, hence the chaotic energy, disruption to our incumbent systems, and general confusion, dissatisfaction, and uncertainty. As I discussed in an earlier book, we are in the process of receiving, and thus interpreting, a new mode of consciousness. Everything comes back to consciousness. As Terence McKenna once said, 'We need to truly explore the problem of consciousness, because as human beings gain power they are becoming the defining factor on the planet. The questions that loom are, 'Is man good?' and then, if the answer is yes, 'What is man good for?''[4] We are in need of a new cosmology – a new worldview – if for nothing other than to find out what humanity is good for.

And this is where the sacred revival is helping out. Gradually our perceptions are picking up on the notion that the human path is one of creative transcendence through conscious evolution. The journey ahead is unfolding around us. We are *in it*, and so we have no choice but to go along with the ride. The world is already innately spiritualized, every molecule, atom, and quark is an energized presence. It is only our worldview that has hitherto invested in separation, in isolation, concrete boundaries, and uncrossable thresholds – and then finally to an all too human alienation of the soul. The question is not *whether* but *when* we will get around to transforming ourselves in order to correspond with the new energies of the epoch, and how much longer we are to continue struggling against it like scared rats at sea. So the first question is: When are we going to shed our monkey mind?

SHEDDING THE MONKEY MIND

God decided to come down to Earth for a quick look at how his creation was coming along. He approached Earth and happened to look at a big tree full of howling monkeys. As He looked down, one of the monkeys happened to look up and saw him.

The monkey became excited and started to shout: 'I see God . . . I see God!'

None of the other monkeys paid any attention. Some thought the monkey was crazy or perhaps just a religious fanatic. They went on about their daily lives collecting food, taking care of their young, fighting with each other, and so on.

Not getting any attention, our monkey decided to try to get attention from God, and said: 'God, Almighty, You are the Beneficent, the Merciful, please help me!'

In an instant, the monkey was transformed into a man living in his own human community. Everything changed, except for one thing: the monkey's mind. The monkey immediately realized that could be a problem.

'Well, thank you God, but what about my mind?'
'That,' said God, 'you will have to change yourself.'

Historians have noted that for around one thousand years — the period between 500 and 1500 CE — the human psyche showed almost no signs of interiority.

There was little interest in probing into the mind itself within the incumbent socioreligious culture. However, from 1050 CE onwards, monasticism did show signs of interiority and its relation with morals and ethics. This, it is suggested, proved to be anathema to the orthodox religious institutions, especially the Catholic Church, as it gave rise to increased Gnostic experience.

Around this time a number of religious sects emerged which had elements of Gnosticism and Manichaeism in their teachings and which were treated as the highest form of heresy. These included such sects as the Bogomils and the Cathars. From firsthand accounts that have survived, it appears that the Gnostic aspect of these sects relied on deep states of *interiority* and vision, and this worried the Orthodox Church. As a result, the Inquisition—a judicial system of the Roman Catholic Church—was established in the late twelfth century to directly combat heresy. As cultural historian Morris Berman notes, such Gnostic discoveries 'are not easily assimilated by a civilization that has been living without interiority for more than five hundred years. . . . As a result, the legacy of the period 1050–1350 has not been a healthy one.'[5] It has even been suggested that the Inquisition can be seen as the origin of the modern police state. That is, the masses are held in check by various forms of administrative violence posing as social institutions.

The mass mind (the monkey mind) of humanity has reacted often aggressively, sometimes bemusedly when essential tendencies are repressed. These tendencies are often labeled as pagan, mystical, heretical, or even downright taboo; and such repressions often resurface in other ways and in other forms. Yet the real Western heresy has been the suppression and denial of such sacred tendencies and Gnostic elements in society. Archaic energy has arisen in many varied forms over the centuries. We can see how the phenomena of Fascism and Nazism in the twentieth century were instances of archaic energy bursting out into social manifestation as a result of giving expression to repressed tendencies and vital energies. Such 'vital force' within humankind has been the source of much investigation, speculation, and surreptitious experimentation. From Henri Bergson's élan vital to the Nazi Party's foray into folk energies, the basis is the perception of a developmental force underlying life's complex evolutionary drives. To be able to tap into this force would not only allow a perspective on essential mechanisms, but, for some, confer power onto the beholder. This, at its core, is also the understanding of magical and occult traditions. And yet it is very dangerous when manifested through the mass monkey mind. The expression of the human psyche, the unconscious, may be detrimental to the person if it is unleashed into a culture that sees no place for it. Thus, our cultures often socially drug us into the consensus reality. The mind unleashed, according to a sacred path, has been the way of the perennial wisdom traditions. Until now it has been the road less traveled.

We have lived our lives with the knowledge that we are human beings. We are something inherently knowable; we can research and discover ourselves. Anthropologists tell us about the development of the human being and human societies. Sociologists describe to us our social and cultural behavior. Biologists study human organisms, including us; and archaeologists describe human behavior of the past. And yet we have very little knowledge on how to be human *becomings*, on how to transcend ourselves. Despite this, as recent as the twentieth century we have been given tools for opening up, exploring, and unleashing the monkey mind. Through psychoanalysis, depth psychology, and then transpersonal psychology, we have finally been able to coax the deep-lying mind into coming out. Or, as psychologist Anne Baring says, 'It has taken untold millennia for the conscious mind and our capacity for self-awareness to evolve out of this unfathomable matrix of the unconscious.'[6]

When we truly examine what lies within we find there exists, as if eternal, an inner urge that strives toward some form of transcendence. Humanity has a built-in urge to transcend, to go toward something it is yet unable to articulate. As a species we have traveled into outer space, we have charted the depths of our great oceans, we have peered into the heart of the atom, and we have witnessed the flash of the 'God particle' — yet we remain largely ignorant of the inner world of humans, where consciousness meets soul, and where communion with the reality matrix is negotiated. The monkey mind of old has kept us isolated from a living, sacred cosmos, as well as keeping us *from ourselves*. The monkey mind has been the true heresy in our midst. Now we are compelled to leave it behind as we venture into a new type of mind. Welcome to participatory consciousness.

TOWARD PARTICIPATORY CONSCIOUSNESS

What we are today is the result of our thoughts of yesterday. And our thoughts of today pave the way to what we shall become tomorrow.
– From the ***Dhammapada***

We cannot truly know our reality *as it is* because when we think of it we already transform it through our very act of observation. We are not part of an observer reality, but a participatory one. As philosopher Henryk Skolimowski remarks: 'The universe is always given to us with our mind contained in it.'[7] In other words, consciousness (and by inference, our mind) is in everything we observe and comprehend. We are woven into the very fabric of our reality matrix, which includes the cosmos (which is a projection of the reality matrix). What we understand and comprehend of the cosmos unfolds itself through our own unfolding consciousness. Nothing then can happen in our reality without participation. We're back again to those fishes swimming in the great water — and we're the fish!

We are compelled to recognize that what constitutes *mind* is not only extended mind but also the awareness that is immanent in, and intrinsic to, our environment. That is, a nonlocal consciousness pervades matter and mind simultaneously; it imbues and sustains both the tangible and the intangible. Connectedness and wholeness are aspects of participatory consciousness, which by its very nature is integral. Integral and ecological thinking is naturally a part of its essence. The human psyche seeks for wholeness, and it is this sense of separation from the soul of our reality which is a root cause of the 'dis-ease' and fragmentation that exists in our world today. A world that cuts the psyche, soul, and the unconscious off from itself is one that divorces humans from their essential nature, and thus from the spirit of nature itself. Philosopher Owen Barfield refers to this state of perception as the *original participation*, which he refers to as an extrasensory relationship between a human and their world.[8] The state of original participation may also be seen in poetic imagination (the world of the Romantics), and in expressions of sensuous identification with one's environment.

Reclaiming the integral mind and reinstating the original participation does not mean we need to abolish everything that we have achieved until now. It is about restoring an understanding that can help us transcend a modern worldview no longer suitable, nor sustainable, for our future. A sacred, revived cosmology and worldview is one where we have a different understanding of wholeness and interconnectedness. These are the integral aspects of a new sacred impulse within humanity. We can finally come to understand that we never just receive reality, we articulate it by participating within it. And by transcending the limits of our older mind, we are pushing back the boundaries upon how the reality matrix unfolds itself. We are in a relationship of mutual feedback and response with our reality, thus our participation in reality is a *response*-ability. Genuine participation is also a form of empathy, and we cannot truly participate in the world unless we take responsibility for it. To put it another way, '*The universe reveals nothing to the unprepared mind*. When the mind is prepared, through its strange magic, it cocreates with the universe.'[9] Nonparticipation with our reality is one of the core causes of the sense of dislocation deep within us, as if we are *estranged* from our homeland.

    The understanding of our participation with reality through mindful consciousness brings in the notion of creativity and human agency, as I explore in the final chapter. Our cosmos *reveals* itself only slightly to the observer, yet she shows many more of her secrets to the conscious participant.

    Now we are entering a new phase in our development as a human species upon this planet. As new phases come into being and the old ways begin to be dismantled, a great amount of creative energy is released. This has the potential for incredible opportunity, as well as disruptive tendencies and times of uncertainty. As

Morris Berman notes, 'In times of breakdown and incipient discontinuity, vision and transcendence — what amount to the gnosis of ascent — become vehicles for fundamental change.'[10] Perhaps that is why we are feeling the uncertainties within us now, as our social and cultural institutions face the recalibrating waves of disruptive change. Liberation of the mind from old ways can bring freshness and freedom as well as a fear of stepping away from the secure, the known. As the Persian poet Saadi said, 'Deep in the sea are riches beyond compare. But if you seek safety, it is on the shore.'

Into the sea we must venture — heretics, come forth!

HERETICS, COME FORTH

The true history of human civilization on this planet is heresy, for heresies have always been the new forms arising. Human development and our evolutionary growth comes through the 'painstaking refinement of consciousness.'[11] In such times of great transition the heretics are often the ones who speak up for the sacred and essential truths within humanity. And when society burns a heretic, it is because they know full well that their own archaic orthodox structures are weakened and open to collapse. History may include seeming discontinuities where repressed, archaic (or even archetypal) energy erupts, yet this is the outward form of an inner sacred and continual energy. The history of our various cultures has been built upon the history of evolving heresies. As new interpretations emerge, the status quo usually absorbs this. When enough new heresies arise, the culture eventually responds to this by adopting, changing, and evolving.

For centuries Western civilization was the epicenter of a developmental energy that manifested in the phases of industrial and technological revolution. This developmental impulse has now gone planet-wide. The Western civilization phase was a springboard to take humanity toward the cusp of a planetary civilization, with globally diverse cultures. The emergence of a radically new culture signifies the emergence of a new, creative organizing energy which influences and arranges the experience of the culture. As a new creative impulse enters a culture, so does it change how that culture perceives the cosmos and how it frames itself within the reality matrix. Our current transitional epoch towards a planetary civilization signals an incredible *age of access* to an active and dynamic stream of wisdom. Yet it will not come about suddenly, for first the outer cultures will need to undergo much shifting and realignment. That is why more heretics are required — to come forth and connect with the sacred energies as they seep through our societies, our popular cultures, our consciousness, and in between each electromagnetic beat of our hearts.

The heretics and the heresies are all one, connected to the sacred energies that flow within humanity. It is the sacred heresy of genuine revolution; the sacrosanct on the guillotine. It is a forceful, loving, and compassionate heresy. It is this essential stream of the sacred that many wisdom traditions refer to and seek to connect with. To go forward, each thing must learn to transcend itself. The sacred is a dynamic force of transcendence. The sacred will never be absent from the world as long as human beings are alive, mystified by the wonders of the world, and seeking for the meaning of their lives.

The sacred revival, as the current phase of this developmental impulse, will throw away the last vestiges of the human 'monkey mind' and clothe itself with a finer consciousness. Pathways have always existed that sought to reconnect the individual with the 'golden' state of finer consciousness. The idea of the 'golden path' exists throughout many traditions, both ancient and modern. From the liquid gold (the elixir) of alchemy, to the golden thread of traditions that make up the perennial philosophy, the underlying goal remains the same: a unification, or return, of the human psyche with the *original consciousness*. Only then can we truly dream our world into being.

Notes

[1] Skolimowski, *The Participatory Mind*, 265.

[2] Skolimowski, *The Participatory Mind*, 85.

[3] Skolimowski, *The Participatory Mind*, 104.

[4] McKenna, *The Archaic Revival*, 165.

[5] Berman, *Coming to Our Senses*, 203.

[6] Baring, *The Dream of the Cosmos*, 19.

[7] Skolimowski, *The Participatory Mind*, 79.

[8] Owen Barfield, *Saving the Appearances: A Study in Idolatry* (Middletown, CT: Wesleyan University Press, 1988).

[9] Skolimowski, *The Participatory Mind*, 82.

[10] Berman, *Coming to Our Senses*, 298.

[11] Skolimowski, *A Sacred Place to Dwell*, 29.

12

LIVING THE IMAGINAL:
DREAMING THE WORLD INTO BEING

Imagination is the star in man.
– Paracelsus

Imagination is the star in man, the celestial and super-celestial body.
– Ruland the Lexicographer

I feel more and more every day, as my imagination strengthens, that I do not live in this world alone but in a thousand worlds.
– John Keats, *A Letter to George and Georgiana Keats*

The imagination is to be the golden pathway to a new cultural hyperspace.
– Terence McKenna, *The Archaic Revival*

As participants in the sacred order of the world, it is up to us how we choose to connect and commune with the reality matrix that enfolds us. We are like fish swimming within the waters of our own existence. And like fish, many of us are ignorant of the medium which sustains us and within which we thrive. Human cultures are nurtured by the quality of their imaginations, by the power of their perceptions, and the ability to express and manifest great vision. Our planetary civilization, with its diverse mix of life and cultures, also exists within a much grander spiral of cosmic dynamics and galactic movements. The scale of this is so immense, so *beyond* us, that we fail to grasp its majesty if we only prod and poke with the rational prongs of physics and mathematics. We are impelled to investigate further with the far-reaching probe of the human psyche, with creative and imaginative curiosity and visionary play. To take the rational route bypasses the magic of the sacred, and drinks at the mechanical well where the water may sustain us but is less sweet.

The semanticist Alfred Korzybski famously said that the map is not the territory, yet in the world of imagination *the map is the territory*. The world that exists for us is the only world which we know of. Our imagination inscribes the territory of our world reality upon the map that, like a palimpsest, contains in its layers all previous conceptions, visions, and worldviews that have emanated from the human psyche over the eons of our self-conscious existence. And from the scratches and indentations of our imagination we catch and lift a corner curtain upon the world of the *imaginal*. The imaginal partakes of the magical, and together they mesh up an array of potential futures. As I describe later, the infamous 'God particle,' the Higgs boson, was found after decades of searching. Yet it had been given life first in the human imagination, and before that its primordial root existed in the imaginal realm. The realm of the imaginal, the *mundus imaginalis*, does not refer simply to the imagination, or to the imaginary. It refers to the potentials, the visions, and the soon to be actualized 'creative plenum' of the imaginative consciousness. It refers to how the reality matrix is influenced to manifest through the intervening correspondence from the creative consciousness. That is, the creative consciousness of the human being acts as a bridge to reach into the imaginal realm — the vibrant home of archetypes and original vision — and to bring these inspired images and ideas into the world through the imagination. As philosopher Jeremy Naydler says:

> Whereas what is imaginary is the product of personal fantasy and may therefore be regarded as subjective, what is imaginal gives access to a transpersonal content that has an objective reality, even though it may not correspond to any historical fact or physical event.[1]

The imaginal realm is that intangible, transpersonal field where our imaginative consciousness negotiates with the manifesting power of the reality matrix that informs our material world. *Coming into being* is a negotiated relation and agreement. As discussed in the previous chapter, there is no observer and observed, there is only mutual participation. The mundus imaginalis is where all is in potential, and our resonance with this realm is a core and inherent aspect of the sacred impulse.

The sacred revival is about conjuring up possibilities based on potentials. As sentient contributors to the participatory mind, we too have a say in how this particular universe *as we perceive it* unfolds before our very eyes. As if on cue, the universe wished to present us with yet another example of our relationship. In February 2016, science announced that it had discovered the existence of gravitational waves, as first predicted by Albert Einstein a century earlier. Sometimes, an imaginal potential just needs time to materialize in the physical reality matrix—our spectacular primordial soup of creative imagination.

The imaginal world guides and defines our pathway through the world just as surely as the geographies and signposts of the outer world. The imaginal realm explores the authentic experience; the direct, intuitive mode of the human psyche. Modern society fears this mode, and has systematically repressed it and worshipped the mask of the false, conditioned personality. That's why disorder abounds in modern culture, because deep down we all feel this fragmentation and dislocation of the self. The sacred revival seeks to redress and rebalance this disharmony by allowing the direct, intuitive mode to operate more directly in our cultures; that is, by allowing a clearer manifestation of the imaginal realm to *come through* human imagination. As the great physician and philosopher Paracelsus said, 'Imagination takes precedence over all. Resolute imagination can accomplish all things.' Wisdom is not a question of belief, nor is it an accumulation of knowledge. It is a reflection of the resonance we have between the imaginal and the imagination, and how we express this through the conscious human experience.

The Romantic poets and philosophers understood this and strived to express the intermingling of nature, soul, and creative imagination. They rallied against the disenchantment and disembodiment of modern rationalism. The Romantics perceived the individual not as a spectator to life's events, but as an active participant in its unfolding. The psyche was something that unfolded from the inside and radiated out into a life of matter. This was contrary to the mechanistic view of life, which impacts us externally and develops the personality.

Samuel Taylor Coleridge spoke of 'the primary imagination I hold to be the living power and prime agent of all human perception, a repetition in the finite mind of the eternal act of creation in the infinite I AM.'[2] William Blake famously wrote: 'But to the eye of the man of Imagination, Nature is Imagination itself.'* There is no fixed distinction between what is transcribed through the imaginative faculties of the human psyche and the workings of the world. Is the subatomic world with its virtual particles any less real than the world of the imaginative mind? Some physicists even consider the subatomic realm as primarily metaphorical.** The spooky realm of quantum physics, with its uncertainty principle and the observer effect, relays a world

---

*   From a letter to Reverend Dr. Trusler (1799).

**   See *Physics as Metaphor* by Roger Jones.

that is the domain of participatory consciousness. It is the realm of the perennial philosophies, the alchemical traditions, and the like. It is a reality where the human psyche does not confront the outer, material world, but is permeated within it. This state of participatory consciousness is where the imaginal realm operates and is also the bridge to our inner psychic landscape. It is also the connection to the energy and art of transformation.

The sacred revival acknowledges and facilitates the processes of transformation. It is in our innate nature to transform ourselves, since human beings are an inherently transformative species. Yet in the absence of an interior reality we target the transformation of our external material world at the expense of a vibrant, rich, eternal, and magical reality within. That is why the great sacred arts and traditions have always existed, to allow us a glimpse beyond the curtain upon a different means of perception. A part of this perennial tradition lies within the act of imagination — a force of will or flash of inspiration that can pierce through and penetrate the boundary between the reflections and the real. Over a period of time, the modern Western world lost touch and became separated from the transformative nature of imagination. Modern Western cultures erased the initiatory paths, and our social tribes became secular and fragmented rather than sacred and whole. The sense of creative communion with an interconnected cosmos was lost, and the modern soul lay as bare as Mother Hubbard's cupboard.

The sacred revival is about reinstating those traditions that seek to establish the correspondences between the invisible and visible realms. It is an involvement—a sensate sympathy—with creative forces between worlds. In other words, the sacred revival seeks to erode the veil of the invisible plane which supports life in the visible realm. In the words of Henryk Skolimowski, 'In every culture there are invisible forces and presences which interact and interfere with the visible realities. They make the deep underlying matrix... .We all live by the invisible. *It is the invisible that controls the visible.*' [3]

There will inevitably be a revival of the occult as a response to the neglect of the vital link between the invisible and visible planes. In this sense the occult refers to those aspects of a magical world where the imaginal and the imagination roam together. The occult, in its various forms, has always existed as a response to a withdrawal of participation with the imaginal realm. The occult has been one reaction against the atrophy of human senses, where reality became trapped within a very limited range of phenomena. When the modern 'consensus mind' rebelled against the positive realities of mystery and enigma and a secular imagination took the helm, many sacred paths disappeared from the public eye. They were not in hiding; on the contrary, they were very much in public life, just only visible to those who had eyes to see. As in everything, it is a question of perspective. The concepts and notions that frame our consensus reality are formulated on an immense set of restrictions, most of which are incredibly insensate.

The loss of connection with the imaginative faculty has estranged us from the music of the cosmic symphony that plays the strings of sympathy and correspondence. This was a music that was well known to those of the ancient world. It is a sympathy/symphony that resonates and connects us with an active interior world. Because we have separated and boxed the interior world, the outer world pushes against us, tooth, nail, and claw. The old mind, devoid of the imaginal link, has sought to dominate the outer world, to dictate and devour it, unscrupulously. The modern consciousness that has guided us to where we are today does not conceive of the unity of the physical and the mystical, of the material and the sacred elements. It does not recognize our communion with the stars — our bodies of stardust, our psyches bent into shape in the furnaces of supernovas. According to Jung, this process of fission, which separated the *physika* from the *mystika*, set in at the end of the sixteenth century. And so the imaginal world seeks to 'come into consciousness' through the imagination, which is the site of our real hunger for meaning.

The world can be magical, or it can be sterile. Shakespeare knew this all too well. And he often used the characters in his plays to embody the subtle layers of the human mind. Hamlet, for instance, saw the world as 'weary, stale, flat, and unprofitable.'* Shakespeare often

---
*   Hamlet, Act 1, Scene 2.

left clues to the theme of his plays in opening dialogue.

The first lines in *Hamlet* are spoken by the character Bernardo who calls out 'Who's there?' Shakespeare, in his study of the human condition, is asking: Who is there? And the reply comes from the second character, Francisco, who admits that he is 'sick at heart,' or rather, sick in the soul, one suspects. The human condition represented in *Hamlet* is revealed to us as a mirror, or rather perhaps it is a code.

The imaginal realm that seeds our creative world into being not only comes to us through art but also through code. The idea that our reality matrix is a simulation (which is a Gnostic-coded world) has been philosophized by Nick Bostrom, theorized by Jean Baudrillard, and visualized by the Wachowskis in their Matrix trilogy. Art, such as through the Romantics, has symbolized the world as imagination made real. Now code is the new art that cracks and sizzles with the overflow of the imaginal effervescence. Gamers are a new breed of conscious participants in the constructs of the gaming imagination, which codes our brains and rewires our neuro patterns. We are learning that the 'nature of imagination gives us a more penetrating clue to the understanding of the mind than a hundred neuro-physiological studies.'[4]

Gamers are players in the quantum realm where there are no observers, only mutual participants in the transcendent realm of play. Just as the world is dreamed into being through the interrelation of all its parts, mingling in the sea of a shared reality, so too do gamers unfold their worlds around them. Video game scholar Liel Leibovitz even considers that 'video games, their bad reputation be damned, are a godly medium.'[5] And that sacred medium is the realm of play and invention, where foundational rules allow an almost unlimited number of permutations in a creative cosmos. Dutch theorist Johan Huizinga compressed the theory of play into one simple idea that he called the magic circle — to play is to bring perfection into an imperfect world. In other words, to bring the influence of the imaginal world (perfection) into the realm of play and unfolding that is our daily life (imperfection). The imperfect is the realm that requires our mutual participation as coconspirators and cocreators to manage and direct the malleable and pliable material that forms our reality matrix. We too are coders — coders of the imaginal. Is it not permissible then that 'the future of evolution and of the human species belongs to the mind that can conceive the inconceivable, and then find it out there, in the universe, as the universe and imagination blend together.'[6]

The responsibility for 'gaming the universe' of our reality matrix belongs to those whose interior psyche communicates with the dynamics of the cosmos and who have become receptive to its presence. Yet now we are all collectively being called to commune with the imaginal realm and to dream the world into being. As Jung noted:

> Everywhere at all times and in all cultures and races of which we have record, when the greatest meaning, the highest value of life man called gods or God needed renewal and increase, the process of renewal began through a dream.[7]

The highest value now is no longer the gods 'out there' but the imaginal gods interiorized within and through which we dream into being, and into *play*. This is a journey, a Gnostic journey, of becoming conscious through an increased interiorization of the world. It is also an emergence out of oneself and away from the constricting confines of a literal and material world. It is yet again a coming into being through an alchemical process that births a soul in us and of the world:

> Coming to consciousness, coming to *know* is an alchemical procedure because it can only occur by means of a transformation of the body and of the world. It requires the development of a subtle, imaginal body, a resurrection body. . . . This can only take place in and through the imaginal world.[8]

Through the agency of the active imagination we have access to an intermediate realm that is the imaginal world and through which we can dream our world into being. And through this collective, communal dreaming we also connect, once again, with the soul of the world — the realm of the anima mundi.

Notes

[1] Naydler, *The Future of the Ancient World*, 137.

[2] Quoted in Baring, *The Dream of the Cosmos*, 399.

[3] Skolimowski, *The Participatory Mind*, 269.

[4] Henryk Skolimowski, *The Theatre of the Mind* (Wheaton, Illinois: Quest Books, 1984), 160.

[5] Leibovitz, *God in the Machine*, xi.

[6] Skolimowski, *The Participatory Mind*, 180.

[7] Quoted in Baring, *The Dream of the Cosmos*, 23.

[8] Tom Cheetham, *Green Man, Earth Angel* (New York: SUNY Press, 2005), 67.

13

OTHERWORLDING:
OR A RE-SOULING OF THE ANIMA MUNDI

You could not discover the limits of the soul, even if you traveled by every path in order to do so; so profound is its meaning.
— Heraclitus

The catastrophic event that gave rise to modernity is the loss of the soul of the world.
— Tom Cheetham, Green Man, Earth Angel

When we understand that the longing originates in the soul, new ways of imagining the world have to be sought, and these new ways have to be conscious soul ways.
— Robert Sardello, Forward to Green Man, Earth Angel

The grand project of Western civilization has been to 'solidify' the world; to drive the human mind away from the interior realms, and away from the imaginal world. The mind of modernity — as an aspect of the contemporary world — is lacking in interiority. The interior life is but a shallow backdrop to the deep materiality of the external world that draws us in and thus away from ourselves. The ancient Egyptians bear credit for having produced the first maps, circa four thousand years ago. Yet they were not maps of the physical world, but of the otherworld. They mapped the regions where the soul traveled. Similarly, in the famous *Book of the Dead*, the Egyptians mapped the journey of the soul in its transformation beyond the physical world. As well as constructing great monuments of stone in the physical world, they also sought to construct passage through the world beyond our senses. And yet today, the largely Western project to 'solidify' the world meant that the participatory consciousness had to be marginalized, discredited, and finally ignored.

The sacred reality, however, is one where the gods not only exist autonomous to humans, but are also psychic factors within human awareness. The ancient Egyptians, for example, were aware that the deities could infuse and permeate a human being and illuminate their inner world. The sacred reality allowed for the intimate consorting between the human and divine worlds—a coalescence of *otherworlding*. Yet over the course of Western history, from the ancient to the modern world, there have been fundamental shifts in how we have perceived the connection and communion between ourselves and the world. In the far distant past people were aware they lived in a sacred order where, as Anne Baring wrote, 'hidden beings, intermediaries between earth and heaven, still connected the dimension of the physical world to the unseen dimension which ensouled it. There was no rigid line drawn between what was imagination and what was reality, because what was imagined *was* reality. The human soul was part of the greater Soul of the Cosmos.'[1] In the ancient world the world soul—or anima mundi—was very real.

For Plato, the world soul was the interrelated patterns from which the cosmos unfolded. Yet Plotinus is perhaps the philosopher most closely connected with the notion of the world soul. Plotinus viewed all reality as essentially spiritual, and the source of the cosmos as unlimited and infinite. The name he most often gave to this unlimited source, when he was forced to use language, was 'the One.' It symbolized the simplicity of unity; that which lies beyond our descriptions, our categories, our divisions, and our humanness. From 'the One' emanates the nous, the universal principle of the mind. Yet this is not referring to the mind that is manifested within us (the small mind); but rather it is us, and everything else, that exists within the greater mind. We are all rooted within this universal matrix of intelligence—it is our sea of existence, awareness, and knowing. For Plotinus, all patterns of intelligence and order were embedded in the nous, and the nous is what shapes the fabric of perceived reality. The nous, the universal mind, then emanates out into the world soul forming a continuity with no division. In Plotinus's schema, the immaterial world soul then gives birth to nature, a reality brought into being and animated by the world soul, which is itself an emanation from nous—and all belonging within the matrix of 'the One.' It is a harmonious unity of order, pattern, entanglement, and beauty.

The role of philosophy for Plotinus, often called the father of Neoplatonism, was to remember our essential nature, and to awaken us to our true inner vision.

That is, to be able to view the world as it truly is rather than through the collection of things that are secondary in the world. Plotinus wanted to compel us to break through and awaken to a purity of perception and understanding. This is in alignment with the ancient Greek mystery traditions that viewed nature as alive, dynamic, and permeated by a spirit that was open to transformation. Greek philosophers, such as the Stoics, also taught something similar, which on the surface seems to be a mix of animism and alchemy. The 'Great Work' of the alchemical tradition treated matter and soul as being emanations from the same underlying source. A transformation in matter could be possible, yet required the experimenter to totally immerse themselves into the transformational process. Soul and matter mingled within the same matrix, the crucible of purification, where transformation upon an energetic level could be achieved. The boundaries and distinctions of matter and spirit blurred in a sacred art, a tradition, that sought the spiritualization of matter and soul—a sort of fusion within the womb of the world soul.

The alchemical tradition also emphasizes the central role of decay as part of transformation. The Great Work (as alchemy is often referred to) uses the motto *solve et coagula,* or 'dissolve and recombine,' suggesting that the old patterns must first come apart, or be taken apart, before the new can emerge. It is a clear process of transition, of recalibrating states. It also shows that an immersion is required—a harmonious communion with the patterns, relations, and correspondences woven into the matrix of the world soul. Alchemy is not a chemical procedure any more than a menu is the meal. The alchemical tradition clearly understood the engagement between the states of matter, spirit, and minds within the overarching unity of the world soul, which is itself an emanation from the cosmic source, the 'One.'

The Great Work focuses on recovering the lost lunar/feminine sense of participatory consciousness and awareness, and applying it to our lives within the reality matrix. This tradition does not endorse the path of withdrawal or asceticism but, on the contrary, encourages an engagement with the physical world where spirit dwells within materiality. The spiritual and the sacred arises from matter and is transformed and purified while in a material state in order for the spiritual impulse to emerge, manifest, and radiate within our physical world. It is the sacred revitalized and brought into play in the fields of the lord. This is the essence of any true sacred revival—to bring forth the spiritual impulse into manifestation *in* our world. That is, to be *of* the world yet *not* of the world.

The alchemical tradition's focus on 'dissolve and recombine' is reflected in the image of the alchemical symbol of the king: The 'Old King' must die to allow the 'Young King' to live. As Anne Baring notes:

> We can also identify the Old King with an outworn image of spirit that needs to be relinquished in order for a new image — the Young King — to emerge from the depths of the soul. Just as from time to time, we have to buy new clothes to replace worn out ones, so an image of spirit or God which has long presided over a civilization may need to die in order for a new image of spirit to come into manifestation. The King's Son in the above text personifies the different values generated by a deeper relationship with spirit, based on experience rather than belief.[2]

Modernity has been like Eliot's *The Waste Land*, or the Fisher King's perpetual winter, collectively estranging us from the soul of the world. We have lost touch with the Holy Grail and turned it into Hollywood fantasy and computer-generated imagery. The sacred revival is calling us back toward the stellar consciousness, the consciousness that alchemists called the fruit of the inner marriage between the invisible cosmic realm and the phenomenal world. We are being called back to the deep seat of soul that the greatest poets, shamans, and visionaries, as well as artists, musicians, and mystics of all cultures, have connected us to for eons.

The sacred revival lets us know that matter too can be evolutionary, and not just static and inert. Humanity, likewise, is a physical species embedded within an evolutionary impulse that is entangled within cosmic, developmental processes. We are part of the grand play of primordial unfolding and refolding. Or, in the words of physicist David Bohm, we are part of the implicate order and explicate order that form the underlying patterns of the quantum realm. To bring the world soul into manifestation is both a sacred art and a sacred act. It is nothing less than part of our own essential evolutionary flow. We are the surfers that ride upon the great waves of a world-in-soul, a reality ensouled. We are the creative participants, the participatory consciousness, in this essential unfolding and refolding. As Llewellyn Vaughan-Lee wrote:

> The World Soul is not just a psychological or philosophical concept. It is a living spiritual substance within us and around us. Just as the individual soul pervades the whole human being—our body, thoughts, and feelings—the nature of the World Soul is that it is present within everything. It pervades all of creation and is a unifying principle within the world.[3]

As the energies of the sacred revival break through into our lives we increasingly dip our toes into the otherworld. This manifests in our forays into transpersonal psychotherapy, hypnotic regression, holotropic breathwork, fasting, meditation, prayers and chants, music, ecstasy, visioning, trance, dance, medicinal experimentation, and all the rest. From our ancestors' cave drawings to our digital art and virtual worlds, we are, and always have been, otherworlding.

With all our forays into the otherworld, we are now prepared to take the next step in establishing a more permanent communion with the world soul. This will prevent us from being cast adrift in a world of the *other* and instead bring us into a world of *soul*. We must be secured against the loss of soul and rally against the encroachment of a soulless society, which is nothing more than a grand disease. The primary cause of illness in traditional societies is, according to their viewpoint, a loss of soul. Such a soul can be stolen, lured away, made ill by magic, or sold into zombie slavery (such as in Haiti). In such cases, a loss of soul can prove to be fatal. The great psychologist Carl Jung knew better than most when he said:

> People will do anything, no matter how absurd, in order to avoid facing their own souls. They will practice Indian yoga and all its exercises, observe a strict regimen of diet, learn theosophy by heart, or mechanically repeat mystic texts from the literature of the whole world—all because they cannot get on with themselves and have not the slightest faith that anything useful could ever come out of *their* souls.[4]

The sacred revival reminds us that *our* soul is inextricably bound with the world soul, and a loss of one would incur a disappearance of the other. We are now compelled as never before in modern history to engage in otherworlding, to commune with the anima mundi, our mothering soul energy that feeds into the great worldly moon river.

LOSS OF THE ANIMA MUNDI

Where there is no vision the people perish.
—Proverbs 29:18

Patrick Harpur notes that for many in Western society the malaise we suffer from is a loss of the otherworld. In other words, he laments that most of us are disconnected from our vital imagination, and that this severs the connections that give us meaning in our lives. We suffer from what psychology treats as depersonalization—a loss of the sense of self, a loss of inner connection, a loss of communion with one's soul.[5] As the Young King rises we are forced to maintain our essential direction as our civilization, in all its various cultural forms, goes through the process of dissolving the structures and institutions of its age, the dissolution of the Old King. The sacred revival is emerging, not in smooth waters, but amidst the rapids and vortexes of immense change. We are moving through times of cultural and social transformation as structures, systems, and institutions are all in the mix of *solve et coagula* (dissolve and recombine). And yet the essential path has no breaks—it is forever consistent, regardless of external form. Participatory consciousness is pushing through, harking to the collective call of world ensouling.

The repression of the unconscious can also be seen as an attempt to repel participatory consciousness, which is the hallmark of the sacred. Modern life in industrialized societies seems to cause (and cater for) the dissociative state of the human psyche. This disconnection between body, mind, and soul—the rupture of the original, participative consciousness—was central and necessary to a modern industrializing world that sought a mechanized, dispirited workforce. It is no accident that, like an immune system fighting 'dis-ease,' the twentieth century saw the rise of 'interior therapies,' including psychoanalysis first and foremost, as a means of confronting this disassociation of the psyche. Carl Gustav Jung felt that an individual's failure to confront the shadows, the repressed elements in the unconscious psyche, was one of the reasons for the disharmonious state of modern society. Jung recognized that the 'general under-valuation of the human soul is so great that neither the great religions nor the philosophies nor scientific rationalism have been willing to look at it twice.'[6] Depersonalization may be so far ingrained into Western societies and their cult of individualism that many of the consumers of the recent zeitgeist in zombie movies and video games completely miss the in-joke. Art is nothing if not sometimes a subtle reflection of psychic trends (and sometimes not so subtle, too).

The poem hailed as the first great modern poem, titled *The Waste Land* by T. S. Eliot, is a cry against the Western loss of soul. Fellow poet Ted Hughes described *The Waste Land as* 'the convulsive desacralization of the spirit of the West.'[7] *The Waste Land* (our wasteland?) is bereft of any rejuvenating waters. It is a sterile modernity suffering an encroaching desertification in earth, body, and mind. Modern human life is caricatured as sitting out the long hand of winter, awaiting the secrets of spring to unfold and reveal themselves. This spring, these rejuvenating waters, are the soul of the world. The world soul is in us, as we are within it, although until now as largely unconscious entities with a barely visible thread to a world of mythic imagination. As Patrick Harpur puts it:

> Loss of soul is also loss of world-soul, so that he [the individual] is not only estranged from himself, but also from the world, which seems alien and unreal. It is flat, lacking the three-dimensionality that double-vision imparts; and it is dead, lacking the imagination that would animate it.[8]

Yet we are set to move out from the hinterland of psychic shadows. We are awakening to the understanding that there are things which do not *happen*; they always *are*.

Human history has always been intimately entwined within a *psyche* of the world, a world soul, that as a species we both carry, and which carries us. The human species has yet to experience the collective epiphany that we are the world soul. There is neither objectivity nor separation. We are the world soul masquerading throughout a myriad of individual lives. After the *solve* (dissolve) comes the *coagula* (recombine), and this psychic recombination involves the struggle with the dialectical nature of our reality matrix. We are faced with our opposites and yet we must endeavor to recombine them into a state of functional harmony. This process, however, must be taken in its due process, for the unleashing of the raw unconscious may be akin to letting the genie out of the bottle too early. And we know how difficult it is to tame the genie once it is out!

Yet there has always been a tradition that has threaded itself, almost imperceptibly, through human cultures as if a living organism. This is the sacred tradition that protects the heartbeat of the world soul. In the process of dissolving a past reality set (the Old King), a new and different gnosis arises (the Young King) that in wishing to make itself felt sends out ripples and shakes. And that indicates a re-souling of the world.

RE-SOULING THE WORLD

The sacred revival is about renewing and restoring the anima mundi back into the life of humanity. Without it the world will continue to conspire against us. Our air pollutes us, our food inflates and chemically diseases us, our rays irradiate us, and our waters engulf us or evaporate into poisonous puffs. As a global species we have become paranoid of the forces around us, almost forgetting that these very same forces can inspire and animate us. What is likely is that this post-postmodern paranoia is a sign of the world soul reawakening and shaking its sentient atoms back into remembrance. The tree of life is shaking its branches again in an attempt to force us to change how we see the world. Then a re-souled world can revive our collective, imaginative human soul. We are being compelled to fall in love again, and we need to love in order to be loved.

    Love, and falling in love, is a refuge for the ecstatic experience, and where memories of the world soul can find safe harbor. The immersive bubble of love is one of the last mystical experiences freely left to us, and it harbors us from a society of dissolution and decay. The act of falling in love is also a profound inner experience, a genuine expression of inwardness in a world manipulated by regimes of behavior. The fact that emotional intensity can find a relation to mystical transcendence is nothing new. It is little coincidence then that the heretical origins of romantic love entered into the psyche of the West around the same time, and in the same geographical area, as the Gnostic heresies — in the southern part of France, referred to as Occitania at the time, during the High Middle Ages (around 1001–1300). This phenomenon was known as the troubadour movement. The emergence of the troubadours at this specific time and place can be clearly seen as a sacred revival aimed at retaining, channeling, and passing on the inner ecstatic experience. The troubadours brought about a revolution in the way love was expressed, thought about, and experienced. It was a time where an interior longing could be expressed externally in a way never articulated before. It thus created the conditions for others to experience and share in these feelings and conscious expressions. The experience of falling in love was deliberately introduced into the cultural stream of human consciousness, and the experience of being in love was given a structure for its growth and evolution.

Courtly love provided a vessel for bridging interior yearning to an exterior expression. Through this channel other courtly endeavors could arise, particularly in court chivalry, which grew rapidly around the same time. Notably, chivalric ideals were absorbed into literary works such as Chrétien de Troyes' romantic Arthurian legends. Dante's *Divina Commedia* too owes much to this conscious influence. By injecting into public consciousness expressions of longing, desire, the unattainable beloved, and chivalric etiquette, later cultural impulses were seeded. From this have arisen codes of conduct, artistic aspirations, architectural monuments, and various other cultural reminders for the human psyche. It can also be said that the modern day pop song owes a debt to the troubadour influence. Never has the outward expression of a person's love and yearning been so easily achievable to so wide an audience. Such a phenomenon based around courtly and romantic love has indelibly shaped the modern human psyche. As the Jesuit priest Pierre Teilhard de Chardin wrote:

> Love is the most universal, the most tremendous, the most mysterious of the cosmic forces. Is it truly possible for humanity to continue to live and grow without asking itself how much truth and energy it is losing by neglecting its incredible powers of love?[9]

Love *of* and love *within* the world soul is a part of the sacred path that is a living transmission with no religious building, formal structure, or earthly institution—it is revealed through the hearts and minds of people. And when people are gathered together, or in correspondence and communion, they are connected to the world soul, and are ensouling the world.

The sacred is the secret opening through which the boundless energies of the cosmos pour into human cultural expression. It is through the sacred that the imaginal realms bring through the cosmic imagination as an impulse for the evolutionary process upon the planet, and which transforms the physical and cultural conditions of our life on Earth. The sacred revival is a living stream of magic, which infuses everything we know and learn about the world and underlies our very sciences and technology. Re-souling the world is the genuine high science as practical magic.

Notes

[1] Baring, *The Dream of the Cosmos*, 80.

[2] Baring, *The Dream of the Cosmos*, 469.

[3] Vaughan-Lee, *The Return of the Feminine and the World Soul*, 109.

[4] Quoted in Sabini, *C.G. JUNG on Nature, Technology & Modern Life*, 169.

[5] Patrick Harpur, *The Secret Tradition of the Soul* (New York: Evolver Editions, 2011).

[6] Quoted in Baring, *The Dream of the Cosmos*, 360.

[7] Quoted in Harpur, *The Secret Tradition of the Soul*, 309.

[8] Harpur, *The Secret Tradition of the Soul*, 308.

[9] Quoted in Baring, *The Dream of the Cosmos*, 530.

14

BLACK SANDS: HIGH SCIENCE AS PRACTICAL MAGIC

Historians have been wrong in concluding that magic disappeared with the advent of 'quantitative science.' The latter has simply substituted itself for a part of magic while extending its dreams and its goals by means of technology.
— Ioan Couliano, Eros and Magic in the Renaissance

Any sufficiently advanced technology is indistinguishable from magic.
— Arthur C. Clarke, 'Clarke's Third Law'

Magic may not be what we think it is. In fact, it may be very much more. It may in fact be *everything*, and everything that is not magic simply is not. In other words, life itself is magic, and magic never died. Not only the miraculous nature of life itself (and life *is* miraculous!), but also the very process of life creation is itself a form of magic. We live in a world of magic today; without magic there would be nothing. So let's be clear, I'm not talking about white doves flying out of long sleeves, rabbits jumping out of top hats, or sleight of hand card tricks. This is as far away from genuine magic as a tasty meal is from the written menu.

Rather, true magic is about the animation and power of the human soul. The ancient Egyptians knew this well. For them, magic was not so much seen as a series of human practices or rituals, but rather as the essential energy that pervades the cosmos. It was an underlying pervasive energy that humans could access, activate, and potentially direct. The Egyptians understood this magic to be in the form of a god, named Heka, which represented the primal cosmic energy that permeated all levels of existence. It was an energy that animated the bodies of gods and humans as well as plants and stones. Everything was thus instilled with this magic, which was a spiritual energizing power. It was through Heka that things of the material plane could participate upon the spiritual. The spiritualizing force was also the conscious, animating energy. Heka also referred to the activation of a person's soul. The Egyptians believed that one of the functions of magic was to activate the soul within the human body. As Jeremy Naydler notes:

> The ancient Egyptians understood that to become enlightened one must become aware of that which is cosmic in one's own nature. One must realize that there is something deep within human nature that is essentially not of this earth, but is a cosmic principle.[1]

This cosmic principle in one's own nature was magic, or the underlying animating energy of the cosmos.

In those times there was not the vocabulary that is extant today for observing and describing the cosmos.

In the ancient past, which had a participatory understanding of the communion between humanity and the cosmos, language was couched in different terms. The Egyptians, for example, expressed themselves through the visual language of hieroglyphics. In this language the world of humans was inextricably bound with the world of the gods, and thus the otherworld. The deep animating force of the human soul came from a communion with the spiritualizing force of the cosmos. From their language, translated into our own, we know this as magic. Yet to them it was a different form of magic, and totally unlike that which we understand today. And yet if we look at the quirky weirdness of the quantum world, with its uncertainty principle and quantum entanglement, we are seeing the same form of magic that inspired the Egyptians. As Arthur C. Clarke noted, any form of advanced technology is, to the observer, indistinguishable from magic. Magic is the mysterious glue that entangles, connects, communes, and also animates us from nothing to everything. Sacred creation and the creative sacred is the mirroring of the magical quantum collapse into *being*.

The knowledge of sacred magic, of the cosmic mysteries, was sought after by all of our known and most highly regarded historical philosophers. From Plato to Plotinus, such seekers of wisdom traveled widely and extensively in their time to gain and understand such knowledge. Upon their return, they then publicly preached and taught what they had learned. There was that which was allowed to be divulged in public, for the consumption of the masses, and then there were the mystery schools, for those initiates deemed worthy of a deeper knowledge of the cosmos. Magic and natural philosophy were seen as aspects of the same stream of knowledge. It was about the science of material and nonmaterial things; knowledge of the pure forms and secondary forms.

The great religious institutions also openly wrote accounts of the use of sacred magic. The biblical King Solomon was declared as proficient in the magical arts, and it is said that God bestowed upon him the knowledge of the 'true science of things.' In the Quran there are also numerous references to the existence of djinns and their magical and often disruptive influence. Magic is also connected to the cosmos and creation in many cultures, especially in indigenous, so-called primitive tribes the world over. Some form of shamanic contact with the spirit world seems to be nearly universal in the early development of human communities. For millennia it has been known that ritual acts, language, and intention (mental focus) form a bridge of magical influence over forces within the universe. Magic is the art of participation, and the participatory art of communion with the forces around and within us. The celebrated anthropologist Bronisław Malinowski argues that every person, no matter how primitive, uses both magic and science.[2]

Magical practices and religious observances are similar in their approach in that they both employ the manipulation of symbols, words, or images to achieve changes in consciousness. Similarly, both magic and religion often serve the same function in a society. The difference is that magic is more about the personal connection with nonmaterial forces and the power of individual gnosis. In contrast, religion serves to connect both the individual and the community to a prescribed godhead through faith.

Magic in its original form is a practical extension of natural philosophy. Through observation and experimentation it sought to study, and then engage with, the hidden forces of nature. It also sought for an understanding of the relations or *correspondences* between the macrocosm and the microcosm, that is, the 'As above, so below' maxim expressed in Hermeticism. In this sense, magic can also be viewed as an amalgamation of science and religion, which comes from the Latin word *religare*, or 'to restrain.' That is, science seeks to understand, while the religious impulse seeks to bind the human to the greater cosmic forces. Magic was a merging of the natural world with the human spirit. The investigation of nature's secrets, of the cosmic mysteries, was a spiritual quest long before it became seen as a scientific endeavor. As Giambattista della Porta, the sixteenth century Italian philosopher wrote, magic is 'nothing else but the survey of the whole course of Nature.'[3]

THE SACRED REVIVAL

The Renaissance zeitgeist, and especially its magical adherents and practitioners, experienced the world in which they lived as a thriving intelligence, and not just as an intellectual idea. For them, art itself was a form and expression of magic; a means of channeling the secret patterns and energies of the cosmos into the world of matter. The famous German occultist and theologian Heinrich Cornelius Agrippa (1486-1535) referred to magic as 'the most perfect and chief science, that sacred and sublimer kind of philosophy.'[4] The early Renaissance philosopher Marsilio Ficino wrote that, 'The whole power of magic consists in love. The work of magic is the attraction of one thing by another because of a certain affinity of nature.'[5] For Ficino, natural magic reflected a desire to animate human life with the living spirit of the cosmos. Magic then was a means for humanity to align itself with the living intelligence of the cosmos and be able to receive its enhancing energies.
In other words, it was a kind of cosmic connection and download. And when Arabic numerals, now our modern numbers, entered Europe from mainly Arabic thinkers, writers, and speakers, they were adopted quickly by Western occultists. In time these 'uncanny squiggles' came to replace the orderly roman numerals so beloved by government bureaucracy. The vital and dynamic era of Renaissance magic was necessary in laying the foundations for the new Scientific Revolution of the seventeenth century.

In the twentieth century the concept of magic was given bad press by its association with black magic and the public rise of 'black magicians' (or those of the Left-Hand Path). The most infamous of these was the Englishman Aleister Crowley, who preferred the spelling 'magick.' Yet despite his much beloved public displays of antisocial eccentricity and taboo-breaking lewdness, he was a man of deep insight into magical operations. When communicating on a more profound level, he would declare the true definition of magic as being 'the science and art of causing change to occur in conformity with the will.' That is, Crowley used a form of mental and mystical/spiritual discipline in order to train the mind to achieve greater focus in order to commune and participate with the nonmaterial forces of the cosmos. He wasn't so much concerned with the objective possibility of such forces, but rather stressed that by doing certain things certain results would follow. As in science, there was a way to participate with unknown *occult* (i.e., hidden) forces by working out a method of doing things (i.e., inquiry).

Even today various forms of magical practices have merged with accepted psychological principles and are utilized to promote techniques for personal development. For example, the visualization techniques once widely used in magical operations are nowadays often put to use in such diverse areas as clinical psychology and sports training. Many forms of modern recreational health practices, such as yoga, tai chi, yiquan, and qigong, are based on a series of body postures, breathing, and meditation techniques that connect with the underlying energetic force prevalent in the cosmic matrix that surrounds us and in which we are embedded. After all, magic is little more than the application of one's own soul-self, our integral unity, with the cosmos. In other times this would be seen as mystical, magical, and mysterious. And now it is part of the world we are living in as the sacred revival rears its head from the nonvisible to the visible plane once again.

Magic too can be viewed as being indistinguishable from our art, whether we are talking of painting, writing, music, sculpture, or any other medium. Also, the word technology, which comes from the Greek word *tekhne*, means art or the 'science of craft.' Yet as Erik Davis notes:

> Powerful new technologies are magical because they *function* as magic, opening up novel and protean spaces of possibility within social reality. They allow humans to impress their dreaming wills upon the stuff of the world, reshaping it, at least in part, according to the designs of the imagination.[6]

Whether we are talking about magic, technology, art, or science, in the end it is all about the same thing — the exploratory path to knowledge and understanding. And this quest for understanding includes, and often merges, all such forms and pathways. We can say it all constitutes parts of the same body, just dressed up in different rags according to time, context, and culture.

MAGIC AND THE HIGGS BOSON

It is my view that science and magic are manifestations of the same phenomena. There is more than one path or science in persuading the cosmos to open up and reveal her secrets. Science did not overthrow magic; it emerged from it. The beginnings of empiricism were rooted in the magical tradition. It is now well understood that modern chemistry materialized from practical alchemy. Many practicing alchemists, from Paracelsus to Isaac Newton, were employing empirical methods with natural magic. The shift in applications went hand in hand with a changing worldview. Applied science was yet another avenue to gain access to and command the secret forces of the cosmos. What we consider as barbaric and primitive from the past will similarly stigmatize the current methods of our day from a future perspective. We cannot, it seems, escape the trap of being victims of our time.

The underlying basis of science derives from the convictions of the earliest natural (magic) philosophers such as Plato and Pythagoras. Namely, that our apparent changeable world adheres to certain laws that can be applied to external formulae. Is searching for the Higgs boson any different from magical correspondences with nonvisible fields of force? Perhaps applied science then is our modern name for the magical pursuit of eternal truths?

The flame of magical inquiry was also dampened by the rise of religious fervor and cries of heresy. Occult philosophy increasingly found itself confronted by allegations and rumors of demonic flirtation amid the rise of witch trials and mass suspicion (or hysteria). As C. S. Lewis pointed out, the great Renaissance magic was discredited less by science than from a general 'darkening of the human imagination.'[7] Perhaps there is no greater symbolic end to the magical enterprise than the public burning of Giordano Bruno in Rome in 1600. After the demise of Renaissance magic the human imagination did not rise to such heights again until the Romantics. And the depths of the human psyche were not again reached until depth psychology. The new struggle of the human mind was now with the rise of scientific thinking.

Heliocentricity, the understanding that the planets revolve around the sun, came to symbolize the great Scientific Revolution and the step from the medieval mind into early modernity. Our scientists now scorn and smirk at the religious thinking that once placed the earth at the center of the universe, and yet today, centuries on, we know little more than we did then. Our neighboring planets remain as enigmas. Sun flares and coronial mass ejections disrupt our communications and continue to intrigue and baffle us. Dark matter is a mystery that is estimated to constitute 84.5 percent of the total matter in the universe. Dark matter plus dark energy together constitute 95.1 percent of the total mass–energy content of the universe, and we don't know what either is.

The universe is singular, then it's multiple or parallel, it's held together by strings, or it's connected multidimensionally. Or maybe it's a holographic projection from a quantum matrix beyond space-time. We may indeed be in a stage of late modernity, or rather just a later period of medieval-ness. Or maybe, like our philosophical Greek and Arab predecessors, we merely like the fun of being able to 'entertain contradictory worldviews simultaneously.'* As Patrick Harpur astutely observes:

> Whatever we suppress gathers in the unconscious and throws a 'shadow' over the world. Dark matter is precisely the shadow of the imaginative fullness we have denied to our cosmos. The daimons we cannot bring ourselves to admit return as dark 'virtual particles.' Like the psychological shadow, dark matter's massive invisible presence exerts an unconscious influence on the conscious universe.[8]

Renaissance thought and the medieval mind accepted the existence of the world soul, where all things were connected by an underlying force. Modern science banished the soul from roaming the world and replaced it

---

* As noted by Patrick Harpur in his *The Philosophers' Secret Fire*, 171.

with the ticktock of mechanistic laws. The technical inventions of Renaissance science—its clocks, telescopes, and compasses—assisted in trying to discover a new system of universal associations. New correlations, connections, and correspondences were derived by technical means, by the mechanical arts. And yet our high technologies of today are turning this situation around by dematerializing themselves and merging into our environment and our bodies. Perhaps the coming era of high technology reconstitutes a new chimera of the world soul.

Broadly speaking, technology can be defined as those means and devices, both material and immaterial, which allow a greater degree of manipulation over one's environment. Their use also achieves a degree of value for the user. It has often been said that the human species' use of technology began with the conversion of natural resources into simple tools. The prehistoric discovery of how to control fire is frequently cited as one of the first widespread uses of a technology. Whatever definition we choose to use, the essential feature is that technologies materialize magic—they make the unseen magic present in our lives. They bring the sights of the seer into the human eye (telescope), transport telepathic communication (telephone), create harm at a distance (weapons), delve into the mystic heart of the body (microscope), and project our imaginations and otherworlds into image (video). Technologies are an extension of magic by other means.

In this day and age we are moving further into the world of image, as I discussed in chapter eight. We have always been fed images of the world that are not *of the world*. We live in a world of representations, dancing with the shadows on the wall of Plato's cave. We exist in a world that, as Plato would say, is construed from representations of eternal forms. And then we take a further step back as we live in cultures that use symbols and images to relate the represented world to us. We are thus even further away from what is real. There is little wonder then that our souls often feel undernourished. In response, they long for and seek out the sacred, the eternal, and the bridge to the real, and 'the phenomenal is the bridge to the real.' *

Because the scientific revolution put the emphasis on the quantifying eye, the visual aspect became a validating tool of empirical reality. What we could witness became a legitimate part of our truths. 'Seeing is believing,' as they say. What was seen at the end of the telescope or microscope became a new fact to add to the expanding list of facts we kept accumulating. We began to trust too much in what the human eye, and its technological appendices, could see. The eye became a dominant lens for seeking truth within the new paradigm of modern science. This was not the case with our ancestors, who relied much more on close range senses, especially touch and smell, as well as a heightened sense of instinct. Because they formed more of a participatory

---
*   A saying often attributed to Sufi mystics.

bond with the world around them, they did not distance themselves like we do today by viewing the world in terms of object and subject. That is why in modern terminology we refer to the observer effect whereby the act of observation can influence, or make a change, upon the phenomenon being observed.

Quantum physics tells us that through measurement, or rather observation, quantum energy 'collapses' into a particle or wave function. And yet this terminology is misleading as it uses the older vocabulary which stipulated the human eye as a validating tool of empirical reality. It is a fallacy of how we understand sight and observation. We don't *observe* particles or phenomena at a distance — we are already participating in their existence. The observer effect should really be changed to saying the *participatory* effect.

Consciousness is a participatory phenomenon, as I discussed in chapter eleven. In our known reality, we participate in a conscious universe where, according to the Hermetic saying, the center is everywhere and the circumference nowhere. There is no better place for the Hermetic arts and the quantum realm to meet than in the magic of alchemy. This archaic science is the crossroads where science, magic, and the spirit meet. On the material level it is seen as a long series of precise and laborious scientific experiments in order to transmute base metals (such as lead) into gold. It is a play with chemical composition and atomic arrangements, a form of molecular management and interference. However, upon the spiritual plane it is a major magical and mystical arcane participation with nonvisible forces that bind the material world beyond our known sciences.

Perhaps the most well-known and revealing encounter of this process occurred in the twentieth century, according to a written testimony. According to the now infamous encounter, a meeting occurred between the mysterious alchemist Fulcanelli and the chemical engineer Jacques Bergier in June 1937. In a laboratory of the Gas Board in Paris, Bergier was warned about efforts to create the atomic bomb. Jacques Bergier was given a message by Fulcanelli to pass on to the noted French atomic physicist André Helbronner. Allegedly Bergier was told:

> The secret of alchemy is this: there is a way of manipulating matter and energy so as to produce what modern scientists call 'a field of force.' The field acts on the observer and puts him in a privileged position vis-à-vis the Universe. From this position he has access to the realities which are ordinarily hidden from us by time and space, matter and energy. This is what we call the Great Work.[9]

The Great Work, it would seem, involves the participatory mind of human consciousness interacting with a specific field of force that produces a perception of the universe. This appears to be a form of the quantum observer/participatory effect, yet on an intentioned and conscious level—a form of consciously arranged, quantumly entangled perception. This view correlates somewhat with the words of famed theoretical physicist John Archibald Wheeler:

> The universe does not exist 'out there' independent of us. We are inescapably bringing about that which appears to be happening. We are not only observers. We are participators. In some strange sense this is a participatory universe.[10]

Our cosmos is set up for cognitive participation, which is why we should realize that whenever we attempt to observe or describe reality, what we are actually doing is participating, and thus influencing or interfering with it. Our own conscious thoughts are more powerful tools than we realize. In this regard, the 'principle of cognitive participation is replacing the principle of objectivity.'[11]

Moreover, another way of rephrasing the deceptive 'wave collapse' is to refer to it as *coming into being*. What is taking place is a quantum act of creation. The underlying quantum energy landscape of our cosmos is an energetic playing field of participatory creation. It is the ancient Egyptian divine archetype Heka, the spiritualizing force that is the conscious, animating energy of the cosmos. The quantum realm is the magical realm, where through participation the enquiring human mind proposes new hypotheses that then get projected into the underlying energy matrix, which has the potential to conjure them into reality. We could call this the Higgs boson effect, whereby we actually form a participatory relation to the physical manifestations of our own projections.

The Higgs boson was first proposed by a team of physicists in 1964 (and not just one guy called Higgs!). Several other physicists from the 1960s onwards also speculated and hypothesized on the Higgs field effect. This inquiry led to a forty-year search within the international physics community and eventually culminated in the construction of the world's most expensive experimental test facility and the largest single machine in the world — CERN's Large Hadron Collider.*

After many experiments and independently verified research, CERN announced on March 14, 2013, that there were strong indications that the Higgs boson had been found. It was what they had been looking for all along. And finally, after much mental focusing and scientific ritual, with instruments and precise application, a phenomenon materialized into reality. Maybe this is a good time to recap Aleister Crowley's definition of magic: 'the science and art of causing change to occur in conformity with the will.' Was not then the discovery of the Higgs boson an act of magic, after all? Perhaps it will go down in history as one of the most complex, community-led conjuring tricks in the annals of science. Or maybe it will just be seen as yet another proof that the

---

*   Conseil Européen pour la Recherche Nucléaire, or in English the European Organization for Nuclear Research, operates a particle collider that lies in a tunnel twenty-seven kilometres (seventeen miles) in circumference beneath the France-Switzerland border.

scientific method works, which would only go to show, yet again, that the universe exists upon a set of fundamental laws that are just in need of discovery.

It would be heresy to speculate that our quantum reality matrix actually responds to sentient thought and creates, or *forms into being*, material representations of willed projections. If this were the case, then it would be a big secret indeed. So big, in fact, that it would need to be kept hidden from untrained minds who, ignorantly, could set into motion a wave of material phenomenon of destructive and chaotic consequences. Such potential power, if it existed, would likely need to be placed in quarantine until such a time whereby it could be used for the greater good. Luckily for us though, this is only speculation.

Similar speculations have occurred elsewhere too, such as in our popular culture. One example is the science fiction novel by Stanislaw Lem called *Solaris*, which was later visualized hypnotically in Andrei Tarkovsky's 1972 film adaptation. In Lem's story, scientists aboard a research space station are investigating an alien intelligence coming from the oceanic planet Solaris. However, the sentient planet is in turn probing into the minds of the human researchers and investigating them. In this process the planet is able to respond by materializing thoughts, memories, and desires that are deep within the human mind. In this way each scientist is forced to confront those aspects that they have mentally hidden away. By encountering an unknown and alien energetic entity, mental processes are able to be projected into a material reality. The sentient ocean of Solaris could be taken as a metaphor for the quantum field that is increasingly recognized today as a consciousness field.*

While this may seem like magic to us, for the ancestral premodern mind the real magic was the spiritualizing force that animates the entire cosmos. Animation, or bringing something to life, is a spiritualizing force, and it is sacred and magical. And that is why the sacred revival is all about magic: the magic of how we create into being the human soul and project it into the world in which we participate. Genuine magic is the science and art of the participatory mind to commune with the cosmos and manifest our deepest will into materiality. Magic is the spiritualizing force that animates the human soul, and which communes with the soul of the world, the anima mundi. We have also hidden this magic within our sciences, our technologies, and within our human memories and emotions; and yet it is the pervasive force which entangles us all together and from which the immaterial becomes material.

We are finally regaining the understanding through the new sciences that our knowledge is not discovered or given to us but is part of the reality that is being continually created by us. Our penetration into the participatory cosmos is part of a grander unfolding

---
* See *The Self-Actualizing Cosmos:* The Akasha Revolution in Science and Human Consciousness by Ervin Laszlo.

where *everything* is evolving; and our perceptions of the sacred source are evolving as well. The sacred revival is about reanimating our relationship to this profound, spiritual truth, and seeing this as part of how our technologies may be re-defined to empower the human being rather than dehumanizing us.

Notes

[1] Naydler, *The Future of the Ancient World*, 143.

[2] Bronisław Maliowski, *Magic, Science and Religion and Other Essays* (New York: Anchor Books, 1954).

[3] Quoted in Fideler, *Restoring the Soul of the World*, 111.

[4] Heinrich Cornelius Agrippa, *De occulta philosophia libri tres* (Three Books Concerning Occult Philosophy) https://archive.org/details/ThreeBooksOfOccultPhilosophydeOccultaPhilosophia1651

[5] Quoted in Fideler, *Restoring the Soul of the World*, 104.

[6] Davis, *Techgnosis*, 181.

[7] Quoted in Harpur, *The Philosophers' Secret Fire*, 135.

[8] Harpur, *The Philosophers' Secret Fire*, 177.

[9] Louis Pauwels and Jacques Bergier, *The Morning of the Magicians: Secret Societies, Conspiracies, and Vanished Civilizations* (Rochester, VT: Destiny Books, 2009).

[10] Quoted in Skolimowski, *A Sacred Place to Dwell*, 82.

[11] Skolimowski, *A Sacred Place to Dwell*, 81.

15

SEEKING SALVATION:
RE-DEFINING OUR TECHNOLOGIES

There is another world, but it is in this one.
– Paul Éluard, *Donner à voir*

The future enters into us . . . in order to transform itself in us long before it happens.
– Rainer Maria Rilke, *Letters to a Young Poet*

Technology has been a collaborator with humanity upon the sacred path from the beginning. We enlisted technology to help build our temples, our megalithic structures, our towering gothic cathedrals, and our radio signals to the starry heavens. The technological arts and human faith are not in opposition, as many have claimed. They have from time immemorial worked alongside each other at different stages of human development. Often the technological enterprise has been a religious endeavor. As historian David Noble says, 'Today's technologists . . . are driven also by distant dreams, spiritual yearnings for supernatural redemption . . . in an enduring, otherworldly quest for transcendence and salvation.'[1] The enchantment with technology has religious roots that extend further back than the New World conquest, and more than a thousand years in the formation of Western consciousness. In fact, it goes far back into the origins of Christiandom.

THE MARRIAGE OF TECHNOLOGY AND SALVATION

The monastic enclaves were bastions of technological innovation, often hidden behind the high mortared walls of the monastery. In those days what we refer to as technology was called the mechanical arts. In post-Carolingian Europe especially, there was an acceleration in developing the mechanical arts driven by contemplative monasticism. The innovative monastic orders such as Cistercians and Benedictines were involved in developing and improving upon such devices as watermills, windmills, metal forging techniques, mechanical clocks, eyeglasses, and the spring wheel, among others. Monastic work helped spread the idea that the mechanical arts were aids to the spiritual life, which has had an enduring influence upon the European psyche, as 'it encouraged as never before the ideological wedding of technology and transcendence. Technology now became at the same time eschatology.'[2]

The twelfth century leading theologian Hugh of Saint Victor was one of the earliest religious proponents of the so-called mechanical arts and gave them mention in his writings on the classification of knowledge. He also linked the mechanical arts to the salvation and restoration of fallen man. Likewise, the influential Franciscan friar Roger Bacon followed in this tradition in stating that the mechanical arts were the birthright of the sons of Adam and that much great knowledge had been lost in the Fall yet might again be fully revived as part of the recovery toward original perfection as reflected in the image of God. Roger Bacon even went as far as urging the pope to develop new inventions in case the Antichrist should arrive on Earth and seize such new knowledge for his own advantage. Roger Bacon, as well as his famed work on optics, lenses, and weights, was also reputed to have been in possession of the famed bronze head, an automaton sometimes associated with alchemists. Other contemporaries of Bacon include Albertus Magnus and Raymond Lully, both of whom were likewise considered as adept in the alchemical arts. In fact, Lully is now considered by many to be a pioneer of computation theory due to his mechanical system for arranging information. Likewise, in the eighteenth century the inventor, scientist, and philosopher Emanuel Swedenborg married his love for mechanical inventions (such as his flying machine) with his equal love for conversing openly with angels.

The marriage of technology with the religious drive for salvation continued with Francis Bacon who, in the sixteenth and seventeenth centuries, almost single-handedly revived the scientific pursuit. Bacon viewed the development of science as both a technology and a means for redemption, a concept that was mirrored in the Rosicrucians who saw the mechanical arts as a valid path to illumination. These perspectives furthered the medieval identification of technology with transcendence and informed the emergent mindset of modernity. Transcendence is now a common theme within the emerging technologies of the twenty-first century (which seem to have become (mis)aligned with some of our notions of artificial intelligence and transhumanism). This spirit of discovery infused the beginnings of the Royal Society of London, which was founded in 1663 from the more secretive Invisible College.

The Royal Society devoted their resources to many areas of technology including navigation instruments, ship construction, mining, metallurgy, military instruments, and energy devices. Behind the Royal Society flowed a deep occult river of alchemy that embodied the ideal of the 'transcendent knower in quest of the transcendent God.'[3] According to historian Francis Yates, in the 1720s one out of every four English Freemasons was a fellow of the Royal Society.[4] A technologically inspired zeitgeist also flowed through the veins of Freemasonry, which dedicated itself to the 'useful arts' of mechanical invention in the pursuit of a grander human development. Many great technological innovators and engineers came from the ranks of Freemasonry; among the earliest civil engineers in England was John Desaguliers, third Grand Master of the Premier Grand Lodge of England. This spirit of invention also flowed strongly overseas through prominent US Masons (such as Benjamin Franklin). The École Polytechnique in France, which became one of the world's premier engineering schools, was created by a group of Freemasons. Freemasons were the apostles of the religion of technology with ideals of technological transcendence.

One of the most world-changing technological discoveries of our recent era has been the magic of electricity. The word electricity first entered the English tongue in a 1650 translation of a treatise on the healing properties of magnets by Jan Baptist van Helmont, a Flemish physician and Rosicrucian who worked on the borderline between natural magic and modern chemistry. Indeed, as Erik Davis points out, many of 'the earliest books on electricity described the force in distinctly alchemical terms, dubbing it the 'ethereal fire,' the 'quintessential fire,' or the 'desideratum,' the long-sought universal panacea.'[5] And yet now we take it all for granted, how everything we use is plugged into some invisible power grid, as power alternates between positive and negative fifty to sixty times a second. We take little or no notice of how our gadgets also produce electromagnetic fields that mesh with all the other unseen fields in our environment. And yet this 'quintessential fire' has become entrenched in our minds, firing our creative neurons like some energy juice. Erik Davis refers to this as the electromagnetic imaginary: 'Since the seventeenth century, the electromagnetic imaginary has seeped into religion, medicine, and technology,' which has now undergone 'its most remarkable mutation: from energy to information.'⁶ The ever-increasing flows of information are the new magic spells for a world on the cusp of the next stage in transcendence—which includes our outer spaces.

What today we call space used to be known as heaven. Spaceflight is akin to heavenly ascent, which is just a step away from being a technical version of the Rapture (another play on the trope of transcendence). Now our technological prowess is propelling us towards the sacred spaces of the cosmos and its heavenly inhabitants. As Bruce Murray, the former director of NASA's Jet Propulsion Laboratory, declared in 1979: 'The search for extraterrestrial intelligence is like looking for God.'⁷ And now we have the Search for Extra-Terrestrial Intelligence (SETI) as a full-blown enterprise. Interesting to note, although not surprising, is that the first generation of American astronauts all shared pronounced spiritual convictions and held strong religious faith (almost as if meeting with the heavens was closed to atheists). On the 1968 Christmas voyage of Apollo 8, the astronauts gave a Christmas Eve reading from Genesis that was beamed back down to Earth. The holy story of the Creation had been retold and revived through the mechanical arts. And to follow this, Edgar Mitchell (Apollo 14) left a microfilm on the lunar surface containing the first verse of Genesis in sixteen languages. From the story of the Creation to our story of creating, we are moving along the magical spiral of transcending our earlier technologies.

TRANSCENDING THE TIGER

And now we reach out to technology once again as we source new materials, new sustainable practices, and reformed infrastructures to support more ecologically aligned and integral cultures. We need humanity and technology working together toward a more sustainable ecosystem connecting people, lives, and events across the planet. And as human consciousness transcends its older modes and forms, so too will our technologies respond to reflect this new thinking. As discussed in chapter two, Sri Yukteswar's redating of grand cycles of cosmic time indicated that life on this planet has entered a phase in which there would be a distinct increase in the quality of consciousness. Parallel with this would be a greater knowledge of the finer forces at work within the cosmos whereby human civilization would move from the coarser to the subtler modes and means of utilizing the forces available to us. As if a reflection of this, modern technologies are becoming more ethereal, invisible, and blending into our surroundings — literally becoming *occult*. We now need secret code words, a special pass for the initiated, to log into our information clouds in the ether. Our digital passwords have become the new magical spells. The hardware, the physical machine, is no longer the symbol of our time now but is representative of the previous stage. The hard-edged machine no longer casts a magic spell. The spell now being cast belongs beyond the mechanical apparatus and in the intangible yet fluid world of connections, associations, flows, and communications.

The visionary architect Buckminster Fuller expressed a similar notion when he wrote of 'ephemeralization' where he noted the technological trend moving ever closer to the ephemeral: the shift from heavy cables and towers or masts to fiber optics, space satellites, and Wi-Fi. Fuller saw early on how civilization was transforming itself from heavier materiality toward lighter, more subtle forms of connectivity and functionality. Human civilization upon planet Earth has now entered the 'cosmic month' of the constellation Aquarius in the zodiac. The symbol of Aquarius is the water bearer, an image depicting waves of water flowing from the cosmic jug. These are the new waves of energy that shall become our dominant mode of understanding during this cosmic epoch. We are riding upon electromagnetic waves of energy, and more. In this respect, it is interesting that forward-thinking scientist J. D. Bernal, in 1929, envisioned a time when, 'finally, consciousness itself may end or vanish in a humanity that has become completely etherealized . . . becoming masses of atoms in space communicating by radiation, and ultimately perhaps resolving itself into light.'[8]

The ultimate technological transcendence ends in light. Let there be light! For our next step, however, the future landscape is going to seem an alien world to the old linear minds. It may seem like a Japanese man-

SEEKING SALVATION

ga-inspired, digital bardo for the global nomadic tribes of somnambulists. And yet it is all part of the natural blend of evolution upon planet Earth.

Human cultures have always been a hybrid form of technoculture, from the earliest days of making fire, to firing sand to produce the windows through which we view the world outside our abodes. Our relationship has always been entwined, an odd partnership of beauty, betrayal, and the beloved. Neutrality does not exist in a subjective realm. Our technologies are the medium for our messages, and as such they adapt to the changing contexts and content of our world – not always for our, or the world's, benefit. Human civilization on this planet has yet to mature. More magic is required, and more making of the *soul stuff*.

Yet a new Promethean humanity is in the making, illumed by the ethereal, quintessential fire, and driven by the sacred impulse to realize evolution upon the planet along with a sense of our larger destiny in the cosmos. Skolimowski writes:

> Prometheus stands for the eternal myth of the flaming imagination which is continually transcending its own boundaries. . . . The new Promethean fire is the fire of the imagination, the ability to fly beyond, the challenge to our humanity to be reignited, the realization of the full scope of our courage and commitment, the determination of our will to be like Prometheus.[9]

In our determination to be like Prometheus, our greatest benefactor who brought us fire and kindled our love for technology, we are compelled to exhibit a different grade of consciousness. The consciousness that beckons to us now is one that recognizes its symbiosis with its surroundings. It is congruent and fitting with our external flows and extended reach. A new Prometheus is rising, and this time it shall be a collective Titan that gathers together the soulful minds of one species. Fire was our first technology, and we haven't stopped technologizing the transcendent light since. The fire of the gods is part of our evolutionary narrative.

Technology should serve as the empowering link between the world of mind (*noo*sphere) and the world of our cultural artifacts (*techno*sphere), creating another sacred marriage of *technoosis*. In the various X-Laboratories around the world there are inspired innovators creating the next addition to the technoosis. With their secretive whispers, their peculiar customs, shared language, and closed fraternity, they are akin to the monasteries of old. The project of human betterment and transcendence has been ongoing for millennia; it has always been the human sacred endeavor. We must ensure, however, that this sacred endeavor is not hijacked by the shadow forces.

TECHNOLOGY AS EXTENSION OF CONSCIOUSNESS

Technology has emerged as an extension of human consciousness - as a projection of our will to interact, interface, and influence the environment around us as if it were a part of ourselves. Technologies do not arise among human civilization by chance, rather they reflect the state of human consciousness and our ability to perceive our sense of reality. Some technologies may even arise in accordance with our state of readiness to understand them. In a sense, they are a representation of ourselves and reveal our perspectives and insights into how the reality matrix might operate. What I'm suggesting here is that human technologies that are designed to enhance or at least amplify our relationship to the world have an essential and often overlooked connection with the state of human consciousness. Sometimes this innate relationship is out of balance, is lopsided and incongruous, and results in technologies of destruction (such as in warfare, tyranny, and oppression). Other times, the relationship is more aligned and results in creative innovation that aims toward the betterment of human life upon the planet.

Bearing in mind what was presented earlier in the book regarding Sri Yukteswar's redating of grand cycles of cosmic time, there is a high probability that we are entering what Yukteswar indicated as an ascending arc in human civilization. In this time frame, there is a distinct increase in the morality, ethics, and the quality of consciousness in humankind. Along with this comes greater knowledge of the finer forces at work within the cosmos. In other words, civilization moves from using the coarse, heavier materials of gross matter, to managing more subtle, ethereal, and electrical forces of attraction (the 'waves' of the Aquarian water bearer).

If we place this within a recent Western, historical context, we can see that new perceptions of the dimensions of space and time began to birth a psychological consciousness, one that seeks to look beyond the borders and horizons of the physical frontier. The physical expansion of time and space mirrored the inner exploration that exploded during the twentieth century. The early part of the twentieth century was a period when the collective unconscious was becoming a conscious part of the collective mind. These psychological developments coincided with the rise of motion pictures—a way of projecting internal ideas onto the external screen—as a cultural phenomenon.

The previous mindset or consciousness, sometimes called the industrial mindset, was one that viewed the materiality of life as dominant. This was a consciousness of acquisition, possession, ownership, and ultimately control. It was all about who had the hardware, and the power to control the hardware over others. It was an age that flourished on patents and copyright, and restriction and centralization. It was all very tangible — it could be seen, felt, and known. Then technologies started to change. Technologies became increasingly distributed and decentralized as networking became the dominant paradigm and way of operation. All that was solid was now melting into air (to paraphrase Marx and Engels). Also, the spectacular rise in global communication technologies — Internet-enabled devices, digital platforms, social networks, etc. — reflected a new form of participatory consciousness, especially among younger people. With this change emerged also a shift in human consciousness as if, to quote Rainer Maria Rilke, the future had already entered into us.

British historian Arnold Toynbee used his extensive metahistorical study on the rise and fall of civilizations to come up with his 'Law of Progressive Simplification.' By this, Toynbee indicated that the growth of civilization was not so much measured by material resources but rather by its ability to transfer increasing amounts of energy and attention towards nonmaterial growth such as culture, education, artistic pursuits, and well-being. Toynbee also coined the term 'etherialization' to describe the historical process whereby a society learns to accomplish the same, or more, using less time and energy. The next phase is now witness to how unseen information is shared and swapped around the world like invisible electricity — the new Promethean fire. As we can now see quite clearly, human civilization on this planet is transforming from utilizing heavier materiality toward lighter, more subtle forms of connectivity and functionality. It's not happening uniformly yet, although the bubble is spreading and it will allow less technically developed regions to leapfrog over the earlier, heavier phases of technological development. Life on planet Earth is about to increasingly come together through the subtler energies and channels of communion. A new revolution has arisen. Our personal access to technology is now more through the *receiving* and *sharing* of information from and to the ethereal digital cloud that envelopes us.

If we consider how consciousness and the sacred energies are expressed, then there is a pattern. Our reality matrix receives the sacred energies as the imaginal realm filters into our material realm, and consciousness streams into our minds as a received broadcast. So too our technologies are shifting into this mode as part of an overall, integral pattern. These emerging patterns are facilitating a shift from a culture and mindset of acquisition toward one of participation and sharing. This is an energy that supports not control of ownership but collaborative participation. Robert David Steele refers to this mode as the 'Open-Source Everything.'[10] Life on this planet has entered a new beta mode, a new testing phase that will, using computer parlance, include still many bugs and glitches. Yet life has always been in some kind of beta mode, always evolving and shifting into new forms and arrangements. Now we sense that a great frequency has entered into our reality—another phase of experimentation and crossover, with realms merging into other realms. A dynamic and creative energy is pushing and shifting the linear structures to forms that are integrated, restorative, and regenerative, and which moves not in straight lines but in waves, networks, and circles. In other words, the reality matrix is manifesting an energy that has feminine aspects, and which represents the sacred energy. These are the signs of a new species' mind in its infancy.

LIFE IS GOING ASYMMETRIC ON US

In time, as the new energies settle into place, we are likely to see a shift from established institutions to lose networks and social groupings, constituting new asymmetries of arrangement, information sharing, and social relations. Yet in order to arrive there, we will first have to pass through a disruptive transition period where the forces of control and centralization will fight to maintain their dominance. Given time, however, the old forces and patterns must eventually give way to the new energies of the unfolding epoch. The emerging ecosystem of this new epoch will give rise to a new geography where many traditional borders dissolve or are recalibrated and repositioned. After all, ecosystems are innovative and creative and need to be continually nourished and reconsidered.

The sacred view is that nature is not something to separate from, but is rather in organic relation to ourselves, and a shared being in our communal environment. It may not appear to be the case at first as humanity will need time to resettle and rearrange relations. We will need to work out a good, familiar — even familial — relationship. And as in most families, there are territorial quarrels as we grow up. The shifting pattern of energies, as I suggested in chapter ten, are moving from top-down hierarchical flows to more decentralized, circular flows. In this mode, life will appear to be moving at an increased pace, as these decentralized flows facilitate a more fluid interaction and unfolding of events. Change will occur with increased frequency, and time for many of us will feel as if it has been speeded up. All of these changes mark a shift to new models of exchange, away from ownership and toward access. The ecosystem will naturally push toward facilitating individuation (rather than individualism) and create new forms of community and belonging. Social divisions will gradually be dissolved, step by step, as individuals realize that they are empowered actors as part of an increasingly decentralized and collaborative system. The continual transcending of time and space limitations will further encourage and support mobility.

No great technological marvel will alter our human traits - only a shift in human consciousness can do that. And this is already occurring within each new generation coming into the world.* The sacred revival will not sit kindly, or easily, with the older minds of the old-

---

* See my book The Phoenix Generation: A New Era of Connection, Compassion and Consciousness.

er generations. Already many 'older mind' people are feeling overwhelmed by this sudden rush of change and recalibration. The newer generations are being born into a new planetary ecosystem that will feel natural to them, where old lines and frontiers have been fluxed out of rigidity.

This new unfolding ecosystem is not without its pertinent risks and dangers as it is still a recent and innovative playing field. As such, many new players, from government bodies to rogue and extremist organizations, will continue to utilize and experiment with forms of technological control. There are significant opportunities as well as risks since the culture of networking and the sharing economy does not come about without its opposing shadow of oppression and suppression. A different world is emerging and it needs to find its place. Values are being shifted, new modes and ways of doing things are causing disruption, and many things and people are on the move. The planet is shaking, dusting off the older energies, and recalibrating for a new sacred landscape to unfold across its surface and through its shared consciousness. It will not be a smooth process. There is a clash of ideologies and mythologies occurring right now during this labor pain period that are causing damaging instabilities. The emerging planetary ecosystem will inextricably move to address these issues of inequality and corrupt use of power. For now, it remains an open game with an extensive playing field—yet the sacred impulse has its own directional trend.

The new asymmetries of life reflect a continual and consistent change: rapid and innovative change will become a central, essential, and necessary part of future life. The great transition coming into arrangement is not only impacting *how* we do things but also *who* we are in this changing reality. It will impact our sense of identity, how we relate to our fellow humans, and how we understand ourselves as part of the fluid, shape-shifting, 'always on' world around us. There will be raging debates about the quintessential features of human identity. Being human will become a delicate and incendiary subject for some people. No doubt we shall be called upon to trust in our instincts and listen to our interior self as a guiding voice. The reality matrix of which we have been accustomed to throughout our lives is undergoing a radical and monumental shift. There will be many who will resist the changes by wanting to cling to the old forces of familiarity, security, and external dependencies. This always has and always will be the case. Revolutions occur across many different spheres, yet when they come together in a grand confluence then the timer has been set for some radical unfolding and evolving. We must be prepared for an unsettling 'human revolution' as we strive to release ourselves from the older bonds of control and containment.

The next phase of change that the sacred revival will bring to human civilization will compel us to reconsider, and perhaps redefine, what it means to be human. We are not yet ready for 'editing' humanity, not until we understand more about what it means to be human. It's not wise to start one project without being fully committed to the current one. In the years ahead, as human civilization shifts and morphs under a new sacral landscape, we shall be compelled to engage in much interiorizing and soul-searching.

The changes associated with the sacred impulse, and the emerging ecosystem, encourage the strengthening of inspired intelligence — the trust of instinct and conscience in the search for meaning, purpose, and direction. Inspired intelligence manifests aspects of the feminine energies in that it seeks connection, collaboration, consideration, understanding, and imaginative lateral thinking outside of compartmentalization. This is the fluidity entering and affecting the reality matrix. Our physical and digital social, local, and global networks will be ever more important for us, and present in our lives. Whether we choose to manifest things in life, facilitate for others, or nurture others, each involves conscious participation, collaboration, and cooperation. After all, the sacred is nothing if it does not inspire and energize cooperation. Cooperation, which leads to coherence, has been the constant and core driving impulse behind evolutionary trends throughout the cosmos, as I will discuss in the next chapter.

Notes

[1] Noble, *The Religion of Technology*, 3.
[2] Noble, *The Religion of Technology*, 22.

[3] Noble, *The Religion of Technology*, 64.

[4] Francis Yates, *The Rosicrucian Enlightenment* (London: Routledge, 2001).

[5] Davis, *Techgnosis*, 42.

[6] Davis, *Techgnosis*, 41.

[7] Quoted in Noble, *The Religion of Technology*, 134.

[8] Quoted in Noble, *The Religion of Technology*, 175.

[9] Skolimowski, *The Theatre of the Mind*, 140.

[10] Robert David Steele, *The Open-Source Everything Manifesto: Transparency, Truth & Trust* (Berkeley, CA: Evolver Editions, 2012).

16

SACRED RESONANCE:
COHERENCE AS THE COSMIC DRIVER

Incoherence in a system is unsustainable. It is at the root of the incoherence of the human world in our time.
— Ervin Laszlo, *The Self-Actualizing Cosmos*

If the human mind does not loom large in the coming history of the human race, then what is to become of us? . . . The future belongs to the mind.
— Terence McKenna, *The Archaic Revival*

Philosophers, artists, and scientists have been debating for centuries the questions concerning human consciousness, both what it is and how it emerges. Likewise have an untold mass of individuals been exploring the byways of consciousness in their anonymity. Only the more well-known names have left their traces and remarks in the preserved annals of history, yet almost every single individual has tinkered, in one way or another, with their minds. For some it may have been through alcohol-induced ponderings or through drugs or medicinal herbs, while for others it may have been through meditation, music, and musings. Mindful explorations have been undertaken through Rousseauian nature walks, or Petrarchan mountain ascents.

Consciousness is the one thing we swim in continuously and know almost nothing of. And yet it navigates our interaction and our interfacing with the reality matrix. Our world picture of consciousness is the algorithm that dictates how reality unfolds for us — it is the alchemical game designer's secret sulfur. It is the elixir, the philosopher's stone, and the Holy Grail of quests and tribulations. The question, 'What is consciousness?' has sat at the back of our minds like a ghost passenger in our overcrowded chariot of personalities. This question has also been at the heart of many mystical teachings, and approached through investigation and discussion, as well as revelation.

Many a heretic has been burned, hung, or drawn and quartered over how to express one's consciousness. Debates have raged and walls been erected and destroyed between materialistic and spiritual, metaphysical worldviews. And now, thanks largely to the advance of sophisticated scientific methods and technology, scientists have been able to map and study the human brain through observing neuronal patterns, brain disorders, and pathways of human thinking. Yet this has only led to an increased certitude among many scientists of a material view of human consciousness. In other words, consciousness exists as a by-product of the physical brain and thus is a phenomenon that cannot exist without brain function. This is the dominant paradigm shared by most materialist thinkers and scientists.

Yet this dominant paradigm is now being contested by a range of research into nonlocal phenomena, theories of a holographic universe, and life after death experiences. The question of what is consciousness remains open and beguiling. From these renewed scientific insights into the nature of a nonlocal cosmos, new findings have appeared that throw light onto how consciousness may operate. And a nonlocal understanding of human consciousness provides enticing food for thought regarding implications for the increasingly interconnected and emerging planetary ecosystem.

IMPLICATIONS OF A NONLOCAL COSMOS

In the current mainstream model, human consciousness is defined as being generated by the living brain. This is similar to the analogy of a turbine producing electricity. In other words, just as electricity is a by-product of the turbine, so too is human consciousness the by-product of a functioning human brain. This model views human consciousness as being local, as being produced *from* something tangible. Also, when this producer stops functioning—i.e., the brain ceases to function—then consciousness and related streams of experience likewise stop. Mainstream medical science has gone a long way in validating this by-product model of consciousness by repeated experiments on impaired brain function. They are adamant to uphold this perspective which, after all, is a perspective produced from the very consciousness they are studying. Whereas the sacred view has always understood the nonlocal aspect of consciousness, it seems we've had to go full circle in order to recognize it again. In the words of poet T. S. Eliot, cited in the opening of chapter two, 'We shall not cease from exploration, and the end of all our exploring will be to arrive where we started and know the place for the first time.'

The basic premise of this mainstream by-product model is that self-consciousness results from the extreme complexity between the neuronal networks in the human brain. It is, then, a chance consequence of evolutionary biology — or so we are led to believe. This biological theory is therefore not limited solely to humanity, but is applicable to the vast range of living beings on the planet. Yet the level of complexity in biological evolution is, according to this model, represented at the highest level only in humans. Despite the emphasis on a scientifically advanced neurological basis for consciousness, such theories still maintain an orthodox position of consciousness resulting from complexity. For example, neuroscientist Christof Koch, chief scientific officer at the Allen Institute for Brain Science, has publicly stated that 'consciousness arises within any sufficiently complex, information-processing system. All animals, from humans on down to earthworms, are conscious. . . . That's just the way the universe works.' For Koch, consciousness is a by-product of complexity, thus complex systems produce varying levels of consciousness, and 'how much consciousness they have depends on how many connections they have and how they're wired up.'[1]

Another so-called cutting-edge theory from science is 'orchestrated objective reduction,' which was first put forward in the mid-1990s by eminent mathematical physicist Sir Roger Penrose, and prominent anesthesiologist Stuart Hameroff. This theory claims that consciousness derives from deeper level, finer scale activities inside brain neurons. Although controversial at the time, it has now gained greater credibility since the recent discovery of quantum vibrations in microtubules inside brain neurons appears to corroborate this theory. Yet despite such recent examples of new radical scientific theories of consciousness, many scientists still cling to the rationalistic thinking that came out of the Scientific Revolution. That is, consciousness is a measurable phenomenon, something that emerges from a set of causes. In this model there is no room for the sacred, the mysterious, or the pervasive sense of intelligence underlying the cosmos. Rather, consciousness is a secondary phenomenon resulting from primary activity located in the human brain.

Now the mainstream view on consciousness has come under increasing critical doubt owing to a range of experiences that appear to throw suspicion upon its validity. Challenges to the by-product theory of consciousness have come from increasing evidence of after-death conscious experiences. According to the orthodox view, consciousness ceases when the brain dies, i.e., no generator, no current. However, many cases are now proving that human consciousness is maintained even though a person is technically declared brain-dead. The near-death experience (known as the NDE) has been reported by sufficiently large numbers of people who were declared brain-dead. Conscious experience in brain-dead people has been reported in almost 25 percent of tracked cases. The NDE phenomenon has now been widely researched and discussed by many credible sources.[*] Furthermore, this phenomenon is not new and there are accounts of NDEs occurring in medieval times. [**]

The existence of consciousness as a by-product of brain activity in the absence of brain function cannot be accounted for by the mainstream theory. There are also numerous indications that human consciousness exists in cases of permanent death. That is, many years after a person has died their consciousness remains available for contact and communication, whether through chan-

---

[*] Notable examples include Science and the Near-Death Experience; How Consciousness Survives Death by Chris Carter; Dying to Be Me: My Journey from Cancer, to Near Death, to True Healing by Anita Moorjani; Proof of Heaven: A Neurosurgeon's Journey into the Afterlife by Eben Alexander;
The Immortal Mind: Science and the Continuity of Consciousness Beyond the Brain by Ervin Laszlo and Anthony Peake; Return from Death: An Exploration of the Near-death Experience by Margot Grey; and Whole in One: The near-death experience and the ethic of interconnectedness by David Lorimer.
[**] Otherworld Journeys: Accounts of Near-Death Experience in Medieval and Modern Times by Carol G. Zaleski

neling or forms of ESP. However, in these cases the actual person is unable to return to life to corroborate the experience personally. Yet there is now enough credible evidence to put doubt into the mainstream theory that consciousness is solely a by-product of localized brain activity. In order to account for all the accumulating anomalies, an alternative perspective is necessary.

A more likely alternative is that, akin to the sacred understanding, consciousness exists in some way beyond the brain as a nonlocal phenomenon. Using modern computer terminology we can say that consciousness can be accessed external to the brain in much the same way that computers access information in the cloud. That is, consciousness is similar to how information would be conserved on digital platforms accessed by computer networks or other cloud-enabled devices. In this model, the data/consciousness is not lost when the computer/brain is switched off. Memory is a phenomenon that exists beyond the brain, yet can be accessed by the individual or, in some cases, by other individuals. This model allows for not only individual consciousnesses to be accessed and recalled, but multiple ones.

This perspective of accessing multiple consciousnesses beyond our individual one is reminiscent of Jung's collective consciousness. It would also appear to support the observations of psychiatrists and consciousness researchers who have induced altered states of consciousness in their clients. When in altered states, a vast majority of people have the capacity to recall almost everything that has happened to them. Moreover, their recall is not limited solely to their own experience but can also include the experiences of other people as well.* The realm of altered states is a familiar abode for those who have worked with the sacred energies, be they shamans, mystics, or wayshowers. This cloud model suggests something akin to a collective field of consciousness that makes complete information available relative to the mode of access. This perspective shares similarities with the scientific research on the Akashic Field and morphic resonance.** Yet, despite the appropriateness of the cloud theory of consciousness, it too does not account for all observations.

In various recorded accounts of altered state consciousness it appears that contact and access is not only made with traces of one's nonlocal consciousness but also with distinctive, separate conscious intelligence. That is, with an active consciousness that is not the consciousness of a living person. Such experiences, once the realm of shamanic or indigenous traditions, has increasingly entered into mainstream cultures. Previously, such encounters were labeled as mystical or magical, or else they were simply ignored as a quirky anomaly. Howev-

---

* For example, see the work of Stanislav Grof at http://www.stanislavgrof.com.
** For the Akashic Field see Science and the Akashic Field: An Integral Theory of Everything by Ervin Laszlo. For morphic resonance, Rupert Sheldrake's Morphic Resonance: The Nature of Formative Causation.

er, as Western cultures have developed their exploration of the inner realms (such as in transpersonal psychology and similar practices), such experiences have become more widespread and thus need to be accounted for. As discussed previously, these cultural explorations and experimentations are signs of a sacred revival, as technologies of consciousness continue their rise.

Our stage in the ascending arc of Dwapara Yuga is enhancing our mental faculties, clarity of understanding, and knowledge of the finer forces at work within the cosmos. And our clarity of understanding brings us to a remarkable conclusion: that human consciousness can connect, and often communicate, with conscious entities that not only manifest a sense of self, but also carry distinct memories and information. This experience, which can neither be accounted for in the mainstream by-product theory nor the cloud model of consciousness, suggests an alternative explanation—that consciousness is a cosmic phenomenon with holographic qualities.

A hologram theory would suggest that consciousness may manifest in space-time, yet that its source exists in a realm beyond space-time. In other words, consciousness has its origins in a deeper dimension beyond our reality matrix, yet is projected into our quantifiable reality. According to science philosopher Ervin Laszlo, all forms of localized consciousness are manifestations of an integral consciousness that is beyond space-time.[2] The implications of this understanding are that consciousness is not in the brain, produced by the brain, or stored beyond the brain, but is a localized aspect of a conscious intelligence that infuses the cosmos with its source beyond our reality matrix. Such understanding takes us beyond linear thinking and toward an integral, sacred understanding. This sacred perspective recognizes that the brain *receives* and *interprets* consciousness, which is infused throughout the reality matrix, but does not *produce* it.

Conscious thought is thus more about access than it is acquisition. We don't own our thoughts any more than we own the songs we listen to when we stream them from the Internet. We just have access to them, and we personalize their arrangement. We personalize conscious information and categorize it into our likes and dislikes according to our background or social conditioning. This is similar to how we might stream music from the web and create our own individual, personalized playlists. The streaming of digital media and information from the worldwide web is likely to become a permanent feature of our lives precisely because it models how human consciousness operates. It represents the democratization of received information. It reflects the new ecosystem that has shifted from possession to access, as discussed in the previous chapter.

This realization, now increasingly supported by the very latest scientific findings, points toward the materiality of space-time as being a holographic projection.[3] That is, all things which emerge into our space-time are holographic projections coded from a deeper dimension that underlies our reality matrix. The understanding that consciousness belongs to a deeper dimension of reality has been the domain of a long, perennial, sacred tradition that has been embraced by many well-known spiritual figures, artists, and even a handful of intuitive scientists. Now, as part of the sacred revival, it is emerging as the new scientific paradigm for our era. And the evidence for this, it appears, lies in the incredible coherence of the cosmos.

LIVING IN A COHERENT COSMOS

If our observed universe is a projection from an underlying source beyond space-time, as suggested by the hologram model, then we would expect the universe to manifest a marked degree of order. That is, there would be evidence that the reality matrix we inhabit is not the end result of a random assembly of forces. The very latest in scientific investigation is now corroborating the sacred perspective that our universe is remarkably coherent.[4] This coherence, which statistically is far beyond randomness, suggests that coherence is the dominant driver in the universe. From quantum behavior to atoms, complex molecules, and living organisms, coherence appears to be an underlying purpose. There are, it seems, coherent relationships between events from one end of the universe to the other. The universe may not be a fully coherent system, yet coherence appears to be an innate universal orientation. This non-random nature of the observable universe suggests order above chance. Such order has now been scientifically measured in two principle forms: the numerical parameters of the universe, and the alignment (or fine-tuning) of its physical constants.

In terms of the universe's numerical parameters there are a number of coincidences. One of the earliest to be discovered (by Arthur Eddington and Paul Dirac in the 1930s) was the ratio of the electric force to the gravitational force, which is approximately ten to the power of forty. Similarly, the ratio of the observable size of the universe to the size of elementary particles is likewise about ten to the power of forty. There are also other numerical alignments, such as the ratio of elementary particles to the Planck length (which is ten to the power of twenty) and the number of nucleons in the universe.[*] And it doesn't end there. The physical processes that underlie our reality matrix appear to be incredibly fine-tuned. It is not possible within the pages of this chapter to list all the staggeringly precise universal constants that 'just happened' to occur in order for life as we know it to arise in our known universe. Nor would I wish to throw the reader an astronomical, quantum-tuned shopping list of facts and figures! However, one such aspect concerns the expansion rate of the early

---

[*] For further numerical alignments see Ervin Laszlo's "Consciousness in the Cosmos: Part II – The Evidence of Consciousness in the Cosmos" in Watkins Mind Body Spirit magazine, vol. 40.

universe. If the expansion rate had been one-billionth less than it was, then the universe would have collapsed almost immediately. Similarly, if the expansion rate had been one-billionth more, it would have flown apart so fast that matter would not have been able to form.

Another precise fine-tuning exists between the strength of the electromagnetic field relative to the gravitational field. If the difference had been other than it is, stable stars like our own sun would not have formed, nor would the evolution of life have occurred on planets such as ours. Yet another example is the difference between the mass of the neutron and the proton. If the mass of the neutron were not precisely twice the mass of the electron, then no substantial chemical reactions could take place. Our universe has a stable configuration in terms of matter precisely because the electric charges of electrons and protons have an accurate balance. And the list goes on. In other words, our reality matrix is incredibly fine-tuned beyond any possibility of chance. It appears that we exist in a 'just-right' type of reality!

According to the calculations of mathematical physicist Roger Penrose, the probability of coming across such a universe fine-tuned to life by random selection is 1 in 10 to the power of 10,123.[5] Physicist Bernard Haisch has wryly noted that there is a greater probability than this that the universe is teeming with intelligent life. There are no other words for it—the known universe is spectacularly coherent beyond our comprehension. And this drive toward emergent coherence also pervades biological evolution, and is reflected throughout life on planet Earth. The sacred impulses of connectedness and coherence are pervasive throughout our reality matrix.

The intricate elements and processes that make up what we call life all exhibit forms of entanglement that, according to quantum science, show remarkable coherence. Physicists Eric Cornell, Wolfgang Ketterle, and Carl E. Wieman demonstrated that complex molecules, cells, and even living organisms exhibit quantum-type processes (and received the 1995 Nobel Prize for their discovery). What this tells us is that complex organisms could not have evolved on this planet without some form of quantum coherence. Our best friend, the human body, is one example, where each cell produces ten thousand bioelectrochemical reactions every second. Within our bodies there exists a constant flux of interreactions and processes connecting molecules, cells, organs, and fluids, throughout the brain, body, and nervous system.

Recent findings in biophysics have demonstrated that a form of quantum coherence operates within living biological systems through what is known as biological excitations and biophoton emission. What this means is that metabolic energy is stored as a form of electromechanical and electromagnetic excitations. And now this is where things get even more entangled and quantumly spooky. It seems that a quantum-level correlation is not limited to the organisms themselves but also operates between organisms. That is, a complex ecology of organisms exist on this planet that is fine-tuned via coherent fields establishing a biosphere that is interactive and participatory. Life on this planet is a sacred *dance of coherence* between organisms and their environment, with shared access to a participatory consciousness.

Physical, chemical, and biological coherence leads ultimately to a degree of perception and comprehension regarding such relational interconnectivity (Laszlo uses the term 'prehension,' which he borrows from Alfred North Whitehead).[6] What this implies is an element of awareness or conscious interconnectivity between the various subparts of any system. That is, as parts of a given system become more interdependent, there arises a greater degree of emergent perception regarding these interconnected relations. To put this more simply, at some point coherence becomes a conscious purpose. As coherence is the dominant driver in physical, chemical, and biological development, so may it be a significant impulse behind social development.

What I am suggesting here is that a culture or society may display chaotic, random, and disruptive behavior, and yet be governed at an innate and essential level by remarkable coherence. This may, in fact, be a necessity and fundamental prerequisite for not only sustaining life but also for its future development. The implications in this are that social and cultural disequilibrium (including disruptions, chaotic events, and anomalies) may function as tuning adjustments required for developmental potentials in the social environment.

This perspective views social disruptors as mechanisms for adjusting to potentials that allow for greater degrees of coherence. Stated plainly, social disruption and chaotic events could be viewed as physical occurrences that assist in the drive toward greater coherence in the social realm. As such, disturbance and disruption has a role to play in the unfolding of the sacred developmental impulse.

The common trend toward coherence prevalent in our reality matrix is expressed through all the physical realms — the chemical, material, and the biological. This pervasive trend also drives toward emergent conscious awareness regarding interconnectivity. It is speculated that behind this phenomenon exists a conscious intelligence beyond our space-time matrix. Upon this planet the ultimate physical manifestation of coherence may very well be through human social order and civilization. And the peak of coherent human civilization would be at the planetary scale — a planetary civilization. Could this be where immanent universal order meets with an emergent transcendent consciousness? The sacred revival just got a little bit spookier.

SACRED RESONANCE: COHERENCE ON A PLANETARY SCALE

If we allow ourselves a momentary grand sweep of history we will see that the checkerboard shows the rise and fall of countless civilizations, empires, and cultural manifestations. From another viewpoint it will also show a marked shift in the perceptive traits of human consciousness. How we see the world, and our place in it, has always influenced how, and to what degree, we participate in the world around us. And as I've discussed previously, until very recently the consensus had been to view the world as exterior to us, as separate and fragmented. In a historical context, previous empires sought to conquer and control; and to create, as far as was possible, their idea of a unipolar world. Yet no empire ever truly succeeded in this endeavor. Previous city-states, societies, civilizations, and empires have all represented the emergence of groupings, or human systems, seeking greater stability and coherence.

This fundamental need for coherence and stability that came with complex human groupings was often centered on critical resources. The overshoot of a society in the face of dwindling resources often resulted in sudden collapse, as aptly described by historian Joseph Tainter.[7] The drive toward achieving greater levels of coherence within and between human societies, according to this model, would lead toward ever-increasing global interconnectedness and interdependence. And the ultimate scale-up along this trend would be as a planetary civilization. A question that presents itself is: Does the sacred revival represent an emergent developmental impulse toward a planetary civilization? And is this the purpose or drive behind the coherent order that underlies existence in our reality matrix?

Let us begin by taking a small step back. Human civilization has now entered into a period where a unipolar world is no longer possible. The age of one empire dominating the world alone is at an end, despite what we see and hear in the mainstream news! Our present multipolar world reflects a level of deep interconnectivity between the dominant and less dominant nations, states, and regional blocks. Paradoxically, however, this early stage of global interconnectivity and interdependence is creating conflict among the major players, which is the very opposite of what we would expect to see in a drive toward coherence.

So where is the underlying coherence behind this display of social disruption? My sense in this is that coherence is coming in from the bottom up, through our increasingly interconnected physical, digital, and biological ecosystem. Humanity is a vehicle, a channel for extending the mind across the Earth; for animating the integrated ecosystem that embraces the planet like a membrane or living skin. Just as the skin is the largest organ of the human body, the living skin of the planet will be the integrated human-Nature ecosystem that is driven toward coherence through consciousness. As was previously noted, a developing degree of perception of the interconnection between parts of a whole serves as both an expression of coherence as well as a driver toward further coherence. And how we see the world also influences how we interpret our received consciousness. It is likely that the current drive toward social coherence on planet Earth will first emerge through the individual consciousnesses of us, the people. The sacred impulse will push further toward greater coherence uniting the physical, biological, and consciousness realms. It will strive for a greater realization and responsibility within its conscious constituent elements, toward cosmologizing human beings.

Notes

[1] 'A Neuroscientist's Radical Theory of How Networks Become Conscious,' November 2013, http://www.wired.com/2013/11/christof-koch-panpsychism-consciousness.

[2] Ervin Laszlo, *What Is Reality? The New Map of Cosmos, Consciousness, and Existence* (New York: Select Books, 2016).

[3] Ervin Laszlo, *The Self-Actualizing Cosmos: The Akasha Revolution in Science and Human Consciousness* (Rochester, VT: Inner Traditions, 2014).

[4] Ervin Laszlo, 'Consciousness in the Cosmos: Part II — The Evidence of Consciousness in the Cosmos,' *Watkins Mind Body Spirit*, 2015, vol. 40.

[5] Trish Pfeiffer and John E. Mack, eds., *Mind Before Matter: Visions of a New Science of Consciousness* (Winchester: O Books, 2007).

[6] Laszlo, *What Is Reality?*

[7] Joseph Tainter, *The Collapse of Complex Societies* (Cambridge: Cambridge University Press, 1990).

17

COSMIC HUMANISM:
CARETAKERS FOR THE SACRED ORDER

Transcendence is the only real alternative to extinction.
— Václav Havel, Independence Hall, Philadelphia, July 4, 1994

We are cosmologizing the human.
— Henryk Skolimowski, *The Participatory Mind*

We now ask ourselves again, what kind of consciousness is unfolding? We started out in this book looking at how consciousness has gone from the original archaic, sacred mode, to religious, then scientific, and later an industrial, mechanistic consciousness. I suggested that we should recognize how people of an earlier time did not live in the same world as we live in now, nor would they have exhibited the same kind of consciousness as we currently do. Consciousness is not a fixed phenomenon or static expression — it changes alongside the flows and fluxes of history and time.

Western culture arrived to a point in the twentieth century where things unraveled into a postmodern mélange where identity was deconstructed and queried and then more or less left to rebuild itself — or else left in a pile of existentialism. A technological consciousness had begun to emerge rapidly after the successive industrial revolutions that adapted a 'machine style' perspective of control, power, and efficiency; and which eventually propelled global society toward excessive consumption, continual growth, and accelerated dysfunctional tipping points and disruption. This technological consciousness was then beginning to morph into a more fluid, coherent stream alongside a new era of technological innovation. That is, a consciousness that was more in tune with connection, communication, and compassion.

It seems we have gone from worshipping faith, then objective knowledge, to reconciling ourselves with a kind of Gnostic understanding through the subjective self. We atomized, quantified, reified, and alienated ourselves while the sacred took a back seat and looked on, bemused and patient. The return to a sacred vision of the world, as pursued throughout this book, includes its own transcendental seed. Throughout this whole journey, like the sacred hero in the underworld, we have ventured far while within us there remained haunting memories of, and a yearning nostalgia for, some other mode of consciousness. It is a sacred consciousness that is our birthright, and which we have ignored for far too long, suffering the consequences as a result.

The sacred impulse has been present within humanity from the very beginning. It never went away - *we* went away. This situation is similar to the behavior of individuals as observed by psychologist Abraham

Maslow. Maslow noted how people step back from doing something important, believing others will do it instead. Somewhere along the way we made an internal agreement to stay back and not to overestimate our abilities. It appears that too many of us within our dear species have avoided being 'fully human.' As writer Gary Lachman dryly notes, 'In our climate of insignificance, we are more comfortable with the 'only human.'[1] Yet the pressure of the sacred higher mind rests on humanity and does not allow it to remain static for too long but tries to push it ever toward self-fulfillment.

Regardless of how we may feel about it, or wish to rebel against it, the sacred presence in humanity cannot be denied as it is an expression of the evolutionary impulse. As such, it does not stop at transitional stages or before attaining its goal, but is compelled to push toward ever higher states and scales of consciousness. In the words of Terence McKenna: 'We are the children of a force that we can barely imagine. It is calling us out of the trees and across the plains of history toward itself. This process is taking ten, twenty, one hundred thousand years—an instant.'[2] And in this prolonged instant, the long thread of our history, human beings have been deeply involved as participants—at first unknowing, and now conscious. From beginning to the end of it all, the transcendental yearning to go beyond one's present state persists in each of us. All of this, our very *humanism*, has been woven into our human cosmologies.

The creation of our various cosmologies is an inherent and natural human response as a way of experiencing our given reality. The experience of reality is never pure, but always mediated through consciousness in its various states of reception. The cosmology we hold as an individual, a culture, and a species is a reflection of our own state of mind. Unfortunately, humanity has for far too long considered itself separate from the cosmos. As Jung accurately put it, the human feels 'as if exiled on a tiny speck of a planet in the Milky Way. That is the reason why he does not know himself; he is cosmically isolated.'[3] Yet to be truly integrated we must participate in the interests of the human family and of the cosmos at large. In other words, we are compelled to exercise our sacred agency. As Timothy Leary succinctly put it: 'The history of civilization is the history of agentry.'[4]

SACRED AGENCY

The philosopher Karl Jaspers referred to the period from 800–200 BCE as the Axial Age. It was a time that, according to Jaspers, new yet similar ways of thinking appeared in Persia, India, China, and the Western world. He indicated also that the Axial Age represented an in-between period, where old certainties had lost their validity and new ones were yet to emerge. The new religions that arose in this time—Hinduism, Buddhism, Confucianism, Taoism, and monotheism—influenced new thinking in terms of individuality, identity, and the human condition. These new emerging religions helped to catalyze new forms of thinking and expressions of human consciousness. And yet, over time, we have seen how they were not wholly successful in developing coherence in a social context.

Author and educator Duane Elgin has recently referred to our present time as the second Axial Age in that religions of separation are being replaced by a new spirit of communion.[5] In other words, Elgin says that the world is moving into a spiritual communion and empathic connection with a living cosmos. It seems we need reminding that there is nowhere else to go when the cosmos already exists within us. This emerging empathic consciousness that Elgin speaks of is the same sacred energy that I have followed throughout the weaving chapters of this book. It is an energy that actively seeks for conscious participation — and ultimately coherence. The more individual consciousnesses that connect across our planetary networks the greater will be the perception of this interconnectivity, which in turn catalyzes the innate, fundamental drive toward seeking further coherence. This realization of our communion *in* consciousness further initiates the *receiving* of a consciousness seeking to manifest coherence as a universal natural order. In other words, it is a self-referencing feedback loop: the recognition of our participation in nonlocal consciousness amplifies the capacity to receive it, which further expands our recognition of it, and so on.

And now I admittedly shift into a speculative mode. My suggestion is that a specific purpose for sentient human life upon this planet may well be as a driver toward establishing a coherent planetary consciousness. In other words, to be a channel 'bringing in' the consciousness field from outside of the reality matrix into manifestation in our earthly reality. That is, the 'spiritualization' of matter. There is a correlation here with Aurobindo's concept of the Supermind/Overmind, in that a form of higher consciousness can be made immanent upon the material plane. Aurobindo wrote:

> Human evolution must move through a subjective towards a suprarational or spiritual age in which he will develop progressively a greater spiritual, supra-intellectual and intuitive, perhaps in the end a more than intuitive, a gnostic consciousness.[6]

The channeling of the consciousness field would require the preparation of human receptivity in order to actualize this. That is, raising localized aspects of consciousness (individual perceptions and awareness) in order to increase the coherence of consciousness among the whole — a form of *transcendence* in consciousness. And this can be made tangible by local conscious actors, each one of us, becoming aware and participating through our everyday acts of right thinking, right behavior, and right being. This is what I refer to as the 'new human.'

Terence McKenna was touching upon the same theme when he said 'we need to reconnect with the next level of the Overmind — a globally conscious, ecologically sensitive, balanced, human, caring kind of consciousness that we can access only with considerable effort, through self-discipline.'[7] This discipline forms part of the developmental awakening that must work itself through the individual, through perceptions and experiences of life, toward the whole. It is my sense that such development of the sacred energies is blocked if personal understanding remains an individualized concept and does not embrace the universality of humankind.

We are no longer either isolated individuals or an inarticulate mass. We are localized consciousness acting through aware individuals who seek to consciously connect, collaborate, and care about the future. Each one of us, as localized consciousness, is a reflection of nonlocal consciousness; and in this way we are also a reflection against each other - this is the *new human*. Jung recognized that no individual lives within a shell separated from everybody else, but each is connected to all by an unconscious humanity. And as we connect and share our consciousness — our thoughts, ideas, and visions — we will be helping to strengthen the signal or *reception* of consciousness and thus the *bringing in* of a coherent cosmic consciousness. A planetary consciousness upon Earth, as expressed through a sentient, individualized humanity — the *new human* — may not only be a real possibility, it may very well be a fundamental cosmic purpose.

HUMAN PURPOSE IN THE SACRED ORDER

In the previous chapter I discussed how modern quantum science suggests that our reality matrix is coded from beyond the space-time of the cosmos, and as such our reality behaves in a way consistent with what we know as a holographic projection. In other words, the totality of our reality matrix is *in-formed* from a deep consciousness beyond it. The known cosmos thus acts as a whole nonlocal consciousness field, of which sentient life acts as localized manifestations. It has been inferred through various religious and sacred texts and traditions that the universe (material reality) came into being as a way for its source to 'know itself.' This is reminiscent of 'know thyself,' the famous maxim from the Oracle of Delphi. Or, as in the words of philosopher Henryk Skolimowski, 'We are the eyes through which the universe contemplates itself. . . . We are cosmologizing the human.'[8] Self-consciousness is ascribed to those sentient beings at the peak, or greater actualization, of mental development. Self-reflection is one of the prized attributes of self-consciousness, yet how can the whole reflect upon itself?

Self-realization is something we credit to each attained individual consciousness. A realization of the self is part of the path of human actualization. It is a path in which purpose and meaning are core drivers and potentials to be achieved. It is an inner knowing which defies the orthodox scientific view of 'selfish genes.' Human beings, as human *becomings*, are naturally driven by a longing, a purpose, and this signifies a connection or communion with the sacred. Timothy Leary stated repeatedly that human civilization had shifted into an unprecedented era of self-actualization. He says that what we need is self-directed brain change; that is, for new circuits to be activated that are dependent upon internal and external signals.[9]

The psychologist Abraham Maslow, who originated a scale of self-actualization, recognized that one of the characteristics of self-actualizers is that they have far less doubt about what is right and wrong than normal people do, and they act upon this inner knowing. Yet now, as further speculation, I wonder what self-realization upon a greater scale would be like? Self-realization as a planetary consciousness? As a galactic consciousness? And finally, as a cosmic consciousness fully realized and self-conscious through all of its localized manifestations? This would constitute a state of coherence — a *communion* — beyond our imaginative potentials.

Human consciousness is a localized expression of the greater nonlocal consciousness field. As sentient beings we receive aspects of the consciousness that pervades our space-time. We are *animated by it*, and we then manifest this through our own socialized minds and cultures. Our individual expressions of consciousness in our reality matrix also reflect back into the greater nonlocal consciousness field. The greater our individual perceptions and conscious realization, the greater the total realization of the entire holographic consciousness. My sense is that cosmic consciousness is a field matrix that is 'in-formed' through the emerging awareness of each of its conscious subparts. The art of the sacred is that we each have a role in bringing the unfinished world into completion. As Rudolf Steiner recognized, 'Man is not there in order to form for himself a picture of the finished world; nay, he himself cooperates in bringing the world into existence.'[10]

As each one of us wakes up, so to speak, the cosmic net shines that little bit brighter. If enough localized consciousnesses awake upon this planet we may catalyze a localized planetary field into conscious awareness. That is, a planetary field matrix is sufficiently prepared (polished) to bring in the greater consciousness pervasive in the cosmos (comparable to the 'immanence of the Supermind,' in Aurobindo's terminology). In this case, we are each a conscious agent of cosmic realization and immanence. We each have an obligation in our existence on this planet to raise our individual, localized expressions of consciousness. In doing so, we both infect and inspire others in our lives to raise theirs, as well as reflecting back our conscious contribution into the 'original source' of consciousness. In this way we can act as both citizens of the cosmos as well as caretakers for the sacred order – and this is the purpose of the *new human*. The sacred informs us that our reality is not a static state but an active, fluid realm that makes demands on us. As

Gary Lachman says, we need to step up to our rightful place in the scheme of things 'to embrace the obligations and responsibilities that come with being 'caretakers' of the cosmos.'[11] Or, in the words of Terence McKenna, we have to learn to love the alien because we are 'so alienated that the self must disguise itself as an extraterrestrial in order not to alarm us with the truly bizarre dimensions that it encompasses.'[12] Now it is time to bring the alien home, and to bring our home planet and planetary consciousness back to its cosmic home. We are on a path of completion — of conscious completion and communion — which is the eternal path of the sacred. Through this sacred journey of completion we connect and commune with everything else in our reality matrix, and *beyond*. As sacred human beings we can do this; we have always been tasked with this endeavor:

> We can save the universe, we can repair it, take care of it, redeem it and awaken it from its trance by becoming aware of our creative contribution to reality and by intensifying our consciousness to such a degree that we never lose sight of this fact. That is our place in the universe.[13]

We can achieve this through our small acts of conscious participation, and regain our place as caretakers for the sacred order. The emerging technologies and social change upon this planet may well be part of this process, informing an extended mind and empathic embrace across the face of the earth. Magic is alive; magic never died. Everything is ultimately a technology of the soul, and all magic, all science, all human expression is a form of soulful technology. And with each technology we move closer to soulful communion with a grand conscious and sacred order.

The sacred impulse animates the manifestation and expression of consciousness at the individual, collective, and planetary level. And one day we may witness a grand awakening, unprecedented upon this planet, and this may very well be the purpose for sentient life, as conscious agents of the sacred order. The emergence of this 'new human' is likely to be more reality than fantasy. The hidden treasure that is at the very core of our existence wishes to be known — for *us* to be known — by our individual journeys of self-realization. We are not alone. A great planetary future awaits us, as a great treasure that wishes for communion. Welcome to the new story.

> *Truth has to appear only once, in a single mind, for it to be impossible for anything ever to prevent it from spreading universally and setting everything ablaze.*
>
> —Teilhard de Chardin, ***The Heart of Matter***

Notes

[1] Lachman, *The Caretakers of the Cosmos*, 22.

[2] McKenna, *The Archaic Revival*, 31.

[3] Sabini, *C. G. Jung on Nature, Technology & Modern Life*, 13.

[4] Timothy Leary, *Evolutionary Agents* (Berkeley, CA: Ronin, 2004/1979), 12.

[5] Duane Elgin, 'The Buddha Awakening, Integral Expanding, and a Second Axial Age for Humanity,' *Journal of Integral Theory and Practice*, 9(1), (2014): 145-154.

[6] Aurobindo, *The Human Cycle*, 184.

[7] McKenna, *The Archaic Revival*, 11.

[8] Skolimowski, *The Participatory Mind*, 3.

[9] Leary, *Evolutionary Agents*, 52.

[10] Cited in Lachman, *The Caretakers of the Cosmos*, 166-7.

[11] Lachman, *The Caretakers of the Cosmos*, 16.

[12] McKenna, *The Archaic Revival*, 43.

[13] Lachman, *The Caretakers of the Cosmos*, 204.

EPILOGUE

THE LIGHTHOUSE

There was once a man who began building a lighthouse in the middle of the desert. Everyone started to make fun of him and called him crazy.

'Why a lighthouse in the desert?' everybody wondered.

Yet the man would not listen and kept on quietly doing his work. One day he finally finished building his lighthouse. At night, without moon or stars in the sky, the magnificent lightning started spinning its light in the darkness of the air, as if the Milky Way had become a carousel.

And it happened that as soon as the lighthouse began to give her light there suddenly appeared in the desert a sea lit by a river of light, with beautiful ocean-going ships, sailboats, submarines, whales, dancing dolphins, merchants of Venice, the pirate Barbarossa, mermaids, sirens, and many more....

Everyone was amazed, except the builder of the lighthouse, for he knew that if someone turns on a light in the darkness, from the brightness of that light will spring up many wonders.

BIBLIOGRAPHY

Aurobindo, Sri. *The Human Cycle: The Psychology of Social Development*. Twin Lakes, WI: Lotus Light Publications, 1999/1950.

Bache, Christopher. *Dark Night, Early Dawn*. New York: Suny, 2000.

Barfield, Owen. *Saving the Appearances: A Study in Idolatry*. Middletown, CT: Wesleyan University Press, 1988.

Baring, Anne. *The Dream of the Cosmos: A Quest for the Soul*. Dorset: Archive Publishing, 2013.

Berman, Morris. *The Reenchantment of the World*. Ithaca, New York: Cornell University Press, 1981.

Berman, Morris. *Coming to Our Senses: Body and Spirit in the Hidden History of the West*. New York: HarperCollins, 1990.

Brynjolfsson, Erik, and Andrew McAfee. *The Second Machine Age: Work, Progress, and Prosperity in a Time of Brilliant Technologies*. New York: W. W. Norton & Company, 2016.

Burke, James, and Robert Ornstein. *The Axemaker's Gift: A Double-Edged History of Human Culture*. New York: Putnam, 1995.

Campbell, Joseph. *The Inner Reaches of Outer Space: Metaphor as Myth and as Religion*. Novato, CA: New World Library, 2012.

Cheetham, Tom. *Green Man, Earth Angel*. New York: SUNY Press, 2005.

Davis, Erik. *Techgnosis: Myth, Magic and Mysticism in the Age of Information*. New York: Three Rivers Press, 1998.

Davis, Erik. *Nomad Codes: Adventures in Modern Esoterica*. Portland, OR: Verse Chorus Press, 2010.

de Rosnay, Joel. *The Symbiotic Man: A New Understanding of the Organization of Life and a Vision of the Future*. New York: McGraw Hill, 2000.

Dennis, Kingsley L. *New Consciousness for a New World*. Rochester, VT: Inner Traditions, 2011.Dennis, Kingsley L. *The Struggle for Your Mind*. Rochester, VT: Inner Traditions, 2012.

Dennis, Kingsley L. *New Revolutions for a Small Planet*. London: Watkins Books, 2012.

Dennis, Kingsley L. *The Phoenix Generation: A New Era of Connection, Compassion and Consciousness*. London: Watkins Books, 2014.

Evola, Julius. *Ride the Tiger: A Survival Manual for the Aristocrats of the Soul*. Rochester, VT: Inner Traditions, 2003.

Fideler, David. *Restoring the Soul of the World: Our Living Bond with Nature's Intelligence*. Rochester, Vermont: Inner Traditions, 2014.

Guenon, Rene. *The Reign of Quantity and the Signs of the Times*. New Delhi: Munshiram Manoharlal Publishers, 2000/1953.

Harpur, Patrick. *The Philosophers' Secret Fire: A History of the Imagination*. Glastonbury: The Squeeze Press, 2009.

Harpur, Patrick. *The Secret Tradition of the Soul*. New York: Evolver Editions, 2011.

Hollis, James. *Tracking the Gods: The Place of Myth in Modern Life*. Toronto, Canada: Inner City Books, 1995.

Kripal, Jeffrey J. *Mutants & Mystics: Science Fiction, Superhero Comics, and the Paranormal*. Chicago: The University of Chicago Press, 2011.

Lachman, Gary. *The Caretakers of the Cosmos: Living Responsibly in an Unfinished World*. Edinburgh: Floris Books, 2013.

Laszlo, Ervin., and Kingsley Dennis. *Dawn of the Akashic Age: New Consciousness, Quantum Resonance, and the Future of the World*. Rochester, VT: Inner Traditions, 2013.

Laszlo, Ervin. *The Self-Actualizing Cosmos: The Akasha Revolution in Science and Human Consciousness*. Rochester, VT: Inner Traditions, 2014.

Laszlo, Ervin, and Anthony Peake. *The Immortal Mind: Science and the Continuity of Consciousness beyond the Brain*. Rochester, VT: Inner Traditions, 2014.

Laszlo, Ervin. *What Is Reality? The New Map of Cosmos, Consciousness, and Existence*. New York: Select Books, 2016.

Leary, Timothy. *Info-Psychology*. New Mexico: New Falcon Publications, 1988.

Leary, Timothy. *Evolutionary Agents*. Berkeley, CA: Ronin, 2004.

Leibovitz, Liel. *God in the Machine: Video Games as Spiritual Pursuit*. West Conshohocken, PA: Templeton Press, 2014.

Lewis-Williams, David. *The Mind in the Cave: Consciousness and the Origins of Art*. London: Thames & Hudson, 2004.

McKenna, Terence. *The Archaic Revival*. New York: HarperCollins, 1991.

McLuhan, Marshall. *Understanding Media*. London: Routledge, 2002/1964.

McLuhan, Marshall, and Quentin Fiore. *War and Peace in the Global Village*. New York: Bantam Books, 1968.

McLuhan, Marshall. *Counterblast*. London: Rapp and Whiting, 1970.

Mack, John, E. *Passport to the Cosmos: Human Transformation & Alien Encounters*. New York: Crown Publishers, 1999.

Naydler, Jeremy. *The Future of the Ancient World: Essays on the History of Consciousness*. Rochester, VT: Inner Traditions, 2009.

Noble, David F. *The Religion of Technology: The Divinity of Man and the Spirit of Invention*. London: Penguin, 1999.

Ong, Walter. *Orality and Literacy: The Technologizing of the Word*. London: Routledge, 1982.

Pfeiffer, Trish, and John E. Mack, eds. *Mind Before Matter: Visions of a New Science of Consciousness*. Winchester: O Books, 2007.

Sabini, Meredith, ed. *C. G. Jung on Nature, Technology & Modern Life*. Berkeley, CA: North Atlantic Books, 2008.

Schmidt, Eric, and Jared Cohen. *The New Digital Age: Reshaping the Future of People, Nations and Business*. New York: John Murray, 2014.

Schwab, Klaus. *The Fourth Industrial Revolution*. Geneva: World Economic Forum, 2016.

Shah, Idries. *The Sufis*. London: Octagon, 1982.

Shlain, Leonard. *The Alphabet Versus The Goddess: The Conflict Between Word and Image*. New York: Penguin, 1998.

Skolimowski, Henryk. *The Theatre of the Mind*. Wheaton, Illinois: Quest Books, 1984.

Skolimowski, Henryk. *Living Philosophy: Eco-Philosophy as a Tree of Life*. London: Penguin/Arkana, 1992.

Skolimowsk, Henryk. *A Sacred Place to Dwell: Living With Reverence Upon the Earth*. Shaftesbury, Dorset: Element Books, 1993.

Skolimowski, Henryk. *The Participatory Mind: A New Theory of Knowledge and of the Universe*. London: Penguin/Arkana, 1994.

Steele, Robert David. *The Open-Source Everything Manifesto: Transparency, Truth & Trust*. Berkeley, CA: Evolver Editions, 2012.

Tarnas, Richard. *Cosmos and Psyche: Intimations of a New World View*. London: Plume, 2007.

Thompson, William Irwin. *Coming Into Being: Artifacts and Texts in the Evolution of Consciousness*. New York: St. Martin's Griffin, 1998.

Vaughan-Lee, Llewellyn. *The Return of the Feminine and the World Soul*. Point Reyes, CA: The Golden Sufi Center, 2009.

Versluis, Arthur. *The Philosophy of Magic*. London: Arkana, 1986.

Vrekhem, Georges van. *Patterns of the Present: From the Perspective of Sri Aurobindo and The Mother*. Charleston: Van Vrekhem, 2012/2002.

Yates, Francis. *The Rosicrucian Enlightenment*. London: Routledge, 2001.

Yukteswar, Swami Sri. *The Holy Science*. Los Angeles, CA: Self-Realization Fellowship, 1894/1990.

ABOUT THE AUTHOR

KINGSLEY L. DENNIS, PhD, is a full-time writer and researcher. His recent book is *Healing the Wounded Mind*. He is also the author of over fifteen books including *The Modern Seeker: A Perennial Psychology for Contemporary Times; Bardo Times; New Consciousness for a New World*, and the celebrated *Dawn of the Akashic Age* (with Ervin Laszlo). Kingsley is the author of numerous articles on social futures, new technologies, digital culture, and conscious evolution. Kingsley also runs his own publishing imprint, Beautiful Traitor Books – www.beautifultraitorbooks.com.

For more information, visit his website www.kingsleydennis.com.

Beautiful Traitor Books was founded in 2012 as an independent print-on-demand imprint to provide unusual and inspiring books for the discerning reader. Our books are works that delve into various domains whether it is books for children, science fiction, social affairs, philosophy, theatre plays, or poetry. We have books translated into Spanish, French, Portuguese, Italian, and Hungarian. All the books we publish seek to explore innovative and creative ideas. Many of them also tell a good story - stories that have different perspectives on life and on the human condition.

Beautiful Traitor Books is not only about offering the reader entertainment. We also seek to offer something that is like a nutrition; something of value that the reader can take away from the book. Good books function on more than one level. Put simply, we thrive on books that have the capacity to shift the reader.

Come and join the conversation – find out more at:
www.beautifultraitorbooks.com

www.ingramcontent.com/pod-product-compliance
Lightning Source LLC
Chambersburg PA
CBHW021139080526
44588CB00008B/121